BAD KIDS
OF THE BIBLE

THOMAS J. CRAUGHWELL,
AUTHOR OF *SAINTS BEHAVING BADLY*

BAD KIDS

OF THE BIBLE

AND WHAT THEY CAN TEACH US

FAIR WINDS
PRESS
BEVERLY, MASSACHUSETTS

Text © 2008 Thomas J. Craughwell

First published in the USA in 2008 by
Fair Winds Press, a member of
Quayside Publishing Group
100 Cummings Center
Suite 406-L
Beverly, MA 01915-6101
www.fairwindspress.com

12 11 10 09 08   1 2 3 4 5

ISBN-13: 978-1-59233-361-5
ISBN-10: 1-59233-361-3

Library of Congress Cataloging-in-Publication Data available

Book design by Nancy Bradham

Printed and bound in USA

CONTENTS

INTRODUCTION

Brace yourself! The boys and girls you will encounter here are the uber-brats of the Bible, the kids whose conduct is the stuff of parents' nightmares. They murdered. They raped. They committed incest. They mocked God and his prophets. They rebelled against their parents. And one especially famous little vixen asked for an enemy's head on a plate.

Why a book on such monsters? For one reason, it helps Mom and Dad retain a sense of perspective about their troubles with their own kids. Of course you're frustrated by your daughter the fussy eater or your son who considers potty training optional, but look on the bright side—at least they didn't sell their kid brother to slave traders. Besides, it's always more interesting to read about bad behavior than angelic behavior—and it's certainly a more accurate reflection of day-to-day family life.

We humans are complex beings, which explains why even the rottenest kids of the Bible had some admirable qualities. Cain was a self-starter. Jacob was devoted to his mom. Absalom possessed charisma. The Prodigal Son knew how to throw a party. And say what you like about Salome, but you have to admit that girl could dance. Part of the trouble with these kids, and with the others you'll meet in this book, is that they misused their God-given talents or warped perfectly natural impulses in very shocking ways. The desire of Lot's daughters to have a family was good and praiseworthy, but how they went about getting their babies makes your skin crawl. The rape of their sister Dinah stirred up righteous anger in the ten eldest sons of Jacob, but they squandered whatever moral leverage they may have had when they indulged in treachery, vengeance, and the slaughter of innocent people.

Sometimes the parents are complicit in the bad behavior of their children. Because David failed in his duty as a father (not to mention as a king who is supposed to mete out justice) by not punishing Amnon for the rape of Tamar, Absalom took it upon himself to

7

even the score. Rebecca's blatant favoritism encouraged Jacob to commit a cruel deception that robbed his brother Esau and made a fool of his dying father Isaac. And is it any surprise, given the incredibly awful family life of the Herods, that the clan produced generation after generation of horrible children?

Nonetheless, there are lessons to be learned here other than the obvious ones—don't murder your younger brother, don't squander your inheritance on cheap booze and fast women. For five thousand years readers of the Bible have learned that the wisdom of this sacred text is ever ancient and ever new. It speaks to each generation, offering timeless answers and solutions to problems and dilemmas. Even in the shocking stories of the bad kids of the Bible you will find fresh insights into repairing broken relationships within the family—or preventing them from happening in the first place—as well as restoring, deepening, and strengthening your relationship with the Lord.

Each chapter concludes with a series of meditations designed to help readers draw an accessible, useful, contemporary message from some of the most shocking stories in the Bible. For example, the story of Shelomith's son who blasphemed the Name of God teaches us reverence for the Lord and His name, but also offers insight into the sin of discrimination, while reminding us that words can be weapons. Then there is the story of Barnabas' teenage cousin, John Mark, whose short attention span and lack of commitment exasperated Paul and broke up Paul and Barnabas' friendship. The first part of John Mark's story speaks to us because we live in a society where so many people suffer from "commitment-phobia." But the second part of John Mark's story, when he has matured and been reconciled with Paul, is also instructive because it teaches us that spiritual growth takes time—and effort.

There are four or five such lessons at the end of each chapter, and a text or two from scripture to reinforce the message while serving as a jumping-off point for discussion with your family and friends. You could even use these texts for meditation in your daily devotions.

Finally, a word about the bad kids you'll encounter in this book. Some are children, like Manasseh and the boys of Bethel who mocked the prophet Elisha. Others are teenagers, such as Salome, the Prodigal Son, and Jacob. Still others, such as Amnon, Absalom, Adonijah, and Lot's Daughters are young adults. I have expanded the concept of "kids" then to include people from the Bible who are always identified as the son or daughter of X or Y, and whose terrible behavior is a result of how their parents raised them (think of Athaliah and Bernice) or whose terrible behavior did serious damage to their own family (Cain is the classic example, but Hophni and Phinhas, the sons of the high priest Eli, fall into this category, too).

At the risk of stating the obvious, we're not holding up the bad kids of the Bible as role models. These stories are what college literature professors call "cautionary tales": you read about Ham or the Daughters of Moab or Micah the Ephraimite and you know you most definitely should not "go and do likewise."

Perhaps we are so accustomed to turning for wisdom and guidance from the parables of Jesus and the letters of Paul, we may forget that the Bible also sheds light on our day-to-day challenges in the stories of its heroes. And villains. And brats.

So get your favorite translation of the scriptures, gather your friends and neighbors, and brace yourself for unexpected insights into family life and the spiritual life through these stories of twenty-four of the naughtiest, nastiest, most wayward, worst disciplined, baddest kids of the Bible.

CHAPTER 1

CAIN

THE FIRST BAD BOY

Genesis 4: 1–16

The idyllic world of Eden ended when Eve, tempted by the serpent, ate the forbidden fruit. Adam and Eve's children Cain and Abel would never know what their parents' world had been like. But they were the recipients of some of the ugly fallout: sibling rivalry, murder, rebellion against the commandments of God. Cain—jealous, resentful and possessed of an unreasonable sense of entitlement—took his frustrations out on his unsuspecting brother Abel.

Cain and his younger brother Abel were the original self-starters, the initial entrepreneurs, the first self-made men. Cain took up farming. Abel became a shepherd. And as the human population at this time was modest, Cain and Abel had no competition. It was a capitalist's dream.

It was also hard work. Since their parents, Adam and Eve, had been shown the door at Eden, the first family had to earn their living by the sweat of their brows. In this fallen world, Cain contended with thorns and thistles that sprang up among his crops, birds that gobbled up the produce, bugs that swept through the fields, drought one year, floods the next, and all the other troubles that plague agribusiness.

The shepherd's life was no picnic for Abel, either. Sheep need fresh grass to eat and clean water to drink every day. Once the flock had nibbled the grass down to the ground, Abel had to find another green pasture for them, preferably beside still waters. During the migration, Abel had to leave his flock and go after lambs that had strayed, leaving the rest of the sheep vulnerable to attack by wolves, lions, bears, or any of the other animals that, ever since Eve ate the apple, had made the shift from vegetarian to carnivore. When he returned with the wandering lamb an hour or so later, Abel might find the panicked flock dispersed all over the countryside, and the nasty remains of a wolf's mutton supper lying in the tall grass.

THE DAILY GRIND

The world was a lonely, frightening place in those days. In Eden, Adam and Eve had been perfectly happy, completely secure. In the cool of the evening God came down from heaven to walk in the garden and converse with the first couple. Given how grueling their life was outside Eden, the memories of those idyllic days in the garden were hard for Adam and Eve to bear, for every bit of food they put in their mouths, every inch of shelter that shielded them from heat and cold and wind and rain, every scrap of clothing that covered their nakedness required daily back-breaking labor.

What, then, must it have been like the first time Adam wrenched a muscle, or Eve cut her hand? The first burn, the first blister, the first splinter, the first time either of them fell sick—these things must have been terrifying. And to whom could they turn for help? God is the obvious answer. Although He no longer walked with Adam and Eve in that friendly, intimate way they had known in Eden, He was not far off.

Cain and Abel heard their parents recall their days of bliss in Eden, and learned why they had been driven out of the garden. Perhaps that is when Cain first began to harbor feelings of resentment against the Lord. From Cain's perspective, the hardships he and his family endured everyday seemed excessive considering that all his mother had done was pluck one piece of fruit from a tree. Their punishment, according to Cain's way of thinking, did not fit the crime.

13

CAIN: THE FIRST BAD BOY

By the time they were in their teens, Cain and Abel had settled into their life's work. Cain, as the elder, was more physically mature than Abel; given the hard work of farming, he was stronger, too. As for Abel, a touch of boyishness still clung to him.

THE TWO SACRIFICES

In a fallen world the brothers would have known their share of disappointments, but it wasn't all bad news. There were stretches when the flock was safe and healthy, and the harvest abundant. On one such occasion, Abel suggested they make an offering, a sacrifice to the Lord. With stones from the field, Cain and Abel each built a small, square altar, piled dry wood on top, and then went off to select their offering.

When Abel returned from the flock he bore in his arms a lamb, beautiful and unblemished. "Abel brought the firstlings of his flock and of their fat portion," says the author of Genesis. Prompted by a heart full of love and gratitude, Abel took the best he had and gave it to God. With his flint knife Abel cut the lamb's throat, laid the body on the altar, then kindled the fire.

And what of Cain? "Cain brought to the Lord an offering of the fruit of the ground." It sounds like a simple statement of fact, but the understatement of it, the absence of any mention that Cain's offering was the "fat portion," or the best of his harvest, has made readers of the story sit up and take notice for the last five thousand years. How pathetic it looked lying on the altar, that meager pile of bruised fruit and over-ripened vegetables, the handful of stalks of mildewed wheat. The difference between the two sacrifices could scarcely have been starker—and the Lord noticed. From Abel's altar a great bright flame shot up and a thick cloud of smoke rose to heaven. But Cain's good-enough offering smoldered like wet wood, as a wispy puff of smoke drifted down the side of his altar.

Reading between the lines of the story in Genesis, we get the sense that there is an undercurrent of resentment in Cain's case. Unlike Abel, who freely and joyfully gave the best he had to God as a token of his gratitude for heaven's blessings, Cain couldn't get past all the hard work *he* had done, all the effort it had cost *him* to bring in a good crop. God did not figure in Cain's equation, and so he didn't see the point of offering Him anything, let alone the choicest fruits of the harvest.

From Abel's altar a great bright flame shot up and a thick cloud of smoke rose to heaven. But Cain's good-enough offering smoldered like wet wood, as a wispy puff of smoke drifted down the side of his altar.

Apparently this was a grudge Cain had been nursing for some time, and God, who reads the human heart as easily as you are reading this page, knew it. Cain didn't want to make a sacrifice to God, so God didn't accept it.

SIN CROUCHES AT THE DOOR

As Cain turned away from his altar and his shabby, rejected offering, his heart filled with rage. He had squandered time that he could have spent with his crops, building an altar. He had taken food he had produced by himself, alone, and burned it, wasted it, in an empty gesture. And then heaven refused to accept his gift.

At that moment Cain heard the voice of the One he hated above all things. "Why are you angry," the Lord asked him, "and why is your countenance fallen? If you do well, will you not be accepted? And if you do not do well, sin is crouching at the door; its desire is for you, but you must master it."

Like a father trying to calm a child on the verge of a tantrum, God had stepped in to soothe Cain, to urge him to get his emotions under control. But Cain was beyond such an appeal.

And as he turned a deaf ear to God, it occurred to Cain how he could regain control, find an outlet for his anger, and punish the One who had hurt him. He went to find his brother, Abel.

THE FIRST MURDER

Cain found Abel sitting in the shade of a tree, watching his flock of sheep. Since the sacrifice, Cain's face had been contorted in fury, his fists clenched, his whole body taut and ready for anything that would release the tension. Now, as he approached his brother, Cain forced his muscles to relax. He assumed a pleasant expression, and in a voice that sounded as casual and as natural as he could make it, he said to Abel, "Let us go out into the field." Abel stood up, scanned the pasture, and seeing no sign of any wild beast lurking in the neighborhood, left his sheep to take a walk with his brother.

Cain was alone with his brother—that part had been easy. Now he needed a weapon. And there it was, lying directly in his path—a limb from a tree, about three feet long and as thick as Cain's fist. Abel stepped over it, but Cain bent down and picked up the limb. It felt solid, it was not a rotted branch. Clutching the limb with both hands, he lifted it high, and with all his strength brought it down on his brother's head. Abel staggered under the blow, then turned toward Cain, a look of shock and pain and incomprehension on his face. Cain raised the branch and struck Abel again. This time Abel fell to the ground. Cain had never killed anyone before; he did not know how to do it. But he kept beating Abel with the limb until he was sure that the life had gone out of his brother.

Now, it's relatively easy to turn a deaf ear to the strictures of church law, or the counsel of clergypersons, or even the wisdom of the Bible. But if the heavens open and you hear the voice of the Lord Himself, how do you ignore it?

Yet Cain did ignore the voice of God—just as his parents had done years earlier in Eden. By eating the forbidden fruit, Adam and Eve brought sin, suffering, and death into the world. By murdering Abel, Cain set the pattern for all future acts of violence.

THE LESS-THAN-ARTFUL DODGER

Abel was dead. Cain threw the bloody club into the brush, and forced himself to walk away slowly. He could feel his heart pounding, his blood racing through his veins. He had avenged himself, he had punished God, and no one had seen him do it. So, moments later, when he heard the voice of God ask, "Where is Abel your brother?" Cain lied. "I do not know," he answered. Then, in a surprising combination of defiance and avoidance, he shot a question back at the Lord: "Am I my brother's keeper?"

Now the wrath of the Lord flared up. "What have you done?" He asked. "The voice of your brother's blood is crying to me from the ground."

For once, Cain was speechless, and in that silence God pronounced sentence on the world's first murderer. "And now you are cursed from the ground, which has opened its mouth to receive your brother's blood from your hand. When you till the ground, it shall no longer yield you its strength; you shall be a fugitive and a wanderer on the earth."

God had held out to Cain an opportunity to confess and repent, and with his thoughtless, glib answer, Cain had slapped it away.

As punishment God took from Cain what was most dear to him: Because he had befouled the earth with the blood of his younger brother, any patch of ground that Cain tried to farm in the future would turn sterile. And there was one thing more—Cain had to leave his home and become a fugitive and a wanderer, a hard penalty for a farmer who is by nature settled and tied to the land.

But the story doesn't end here. Genesis tells us that Cain married, had children, founded the first city, and that his descendants invented music and metallurgy—an early example of how God can bring great good even out of terrible evil. But Genesis does not say whether Cain ever repented. He might have. There are precedents in the Bible of sinners turning their lives around—the apostle Peter, for example, repented after denying Christ three times, and he was forgiven. Perhaps Cain repented, too.

Then again, he might have lived on, seething with resentment, still wrapped up in himself, still frustrated that he wasn't getting everything he felt was due to him.

WHAT CAIN
can teach us

WEED OUT HATRED AND RESENTMENT FROM YOUR HEART

Who among us hasn't said, "I could just kill him/her/them?" We mean it metaphorically, of course, but hatred is an evil seed that can grow into things far worse, including homicide. It can arise from a grudge we just won't give up, or an old injury we can't stop thinking about. It can be an irrational dislike of someone or even an entire group, nation, or race. It can bubble up to the surface if we feel that our work hasn't been properly recognized or rewarded. Whatever provokes it, hatred festers in the soul waiting for some outlet or release: fratricide in the case of Cain, or more commonly for you and me, nasty, hurtful words that can never be called back.

Whatever you need to do to purge hatred from your heart, begin to do it today. Whether it leads to serious actions or simply festers inside, hatred colors your view of your world, of others, and of yourself.

"Anyone who hates his brother is a murderer, and you know that no murderer has eternal life abiding in him." (1 John 3:15)

GIVE GENEROUSLY AND FREELY, WITHOUT EXPECTATIONS OR STRINGS

Cain went away from the sacrifice angry and resentful—and this is the part of the story we all can relate to. How many times have we felt that we did what we were supposed to do, and yet didn't get the recognition we deserved? Okay, so maybe we didn't do the task as graciously or as well as we could have, or as generously as was within our means. But we finished the job! So where's our handsome reward?

Just as God could read Cain's heart, He can read ours, too. In our good works for God and for others, it's important to examine our motives and give without expectation of a return.

"Finally, all of you, have unity of spirit, sympathy, love of the brethren, a tender heart, and a humble mind." (1 Peter 3:8)

WE ARE ALL OUR BROTHERS' KEEPERS

By setting this story eons before there were commandments, or constitutions, or litigators, the author of Genesis makes the point that a moral code existed from the beginning of time. Cain violated the most fundamental moral principle: He took a human life. By stepping in, by giving Cain a chance to confess and repent, by meting out Cain's punishment, the Lord demonstrated in an unmistakable way that a violation of the moral code is not just a crime against society, it is a sin against God. As children of God, we do owe one another.

"Against whom have you raised your voice and haughtily lifted up your eyes? Against the Holy One of Israel!" (Isaiah 37:23)

LIFE'S BLESSINGS ARE JUST PART OF THE LARGER PICTURE

Success, affluence, good health, comforts, and happiness are all gifts from God. Seen as ends in themselves, or as the result purely of our own efforts, or as something that we deserve, these blessings can become a snare that can make us greedy, selfish, unkind to those who need our help, and unfaithful in our religious duties. It's nice to have the creature comforts, of course; just don't make them the sole focus and measure of your life. Keep these earthly gifts in perspective as they relate to the whole—and be grateful, not grasping.

"I will walk with integrity of heart within my house; I will not set before my eyes anything that is base." (Psalm 101:2–3)

THE LORD READS OUR HEARTS— AND OUR TRUE INTENTIONS

Parents learn from experience the telltale signs that their kid is up to no good—the unusual expression on the face, or the sudden uncharacteristic silence in the playroom are tip-offs that the little darling is attempting an end-run around one of the household rules. The Lord, of course, doesn't have to wait for such outward signs. He is aware of every less-than-virtuous impulse that flashes across our mind. Consequently, trying to rationalize, justify, or tap dance our way out of a situation in which we are clearly in the wrong is an exercise in futility. To God, our motives and our hearts are open books.

"For the word of God is living and active, sharper than any two-edged sword . . . and discerning the thoughts and intentions of the heart."
(Hebrews 4:12)

CHAPTER 2

HAM

WHAT ARE YOU LOOKING AT?

Genesis 6:5–9:29

T he earth had barely dried out from the Flood, and already Noah and his family were misbehaving. After so many years of hard work and hardship, Noah treated himself to more than just a little bit of wine, made from the first harvest of grapes. His drunkenness spotlights the evils of drinking to excess, but as a one-time event it could have been excused. What wasn't forgivable, though, was Ham's mockery of his father, passed out and naked in his tent. And Ham's disrespect came at a high price.

The first-born child bears the burden of his or her parents' hopes and expectations. The adorable youngest child gets away with murder. But what about the kid in the middle? Child psychologists tell us that often the middle child feels unnoticed, unloved, unappreciated, misunderstood. To get attention a middle child will take up extreme sports, or rebel against parental authority, or build a tight circle of friends whose opinions carry more weight than the family's. If any child will try to annoy his Mom and Dad, it is the one born in the middle.

Genesis always lists the sons of Noah as Shem, Ham, and Japheth. Clearly, Ham is the middle child and, although it takes a little time for us to see it, he acts like one.

In the story of the Flood, the sons of Noah play supporting roles: They help their 500-plus-year-old father build the ark; they serve as the world's first wild animal wranglers, rounding up all those pairs of beasts, birds, and "creeping things" and herding them into the ark; and they collect the vast quantities of food and fodder to feed themselves and their animal companions for as long as the world stayed flooded.

The Bible tells us that Noah "was a righteous man, blameless in his generation," and that Noah "walked with God." We don't learn anything about the character of Noah's wife, or of his sons, or of his sons' wives. Perhaps God spared them for Noah's sake. Or perhaps they were righteous enough in their own rights to deserve a place on the ark. Certainly it would be easier to repopulate the earth after the flood with four human couples. Whatever the reason, God judged that these eight people were worthy to be saved and to begin the world anew.

LET'S HOPE SOMEONE HAD INVENTED THE WHEEL

Human depravity that began with Cain's murder of Abel escalated and flourished as the descendants of Adam and Eve were fruitful and multiplied and filled the earth and subdued it. By the time Noah and his wife were raising their family, the Lord looked down from heaven and saw "that the wickedness of man was great in the earth, and that every imagination of the thoughts of the heart was only evil continually. . . . The earth was corrupt in God's sight, and the earth was filled with violence." It had gotten so bad that God wished He had never made mankind, and even regretted having made animals, birds, and all other living creatures. But at the very moment that he resolved to blot out all life on the earth, God also was moved to pity by Noah, a man who had done no wrong. For Noah's sake, God revised His plan of permanent universal destruction; instead, he instructed Noah to build an enormous wooden ship large enough to accommodate his family as well as breeding pairs of every living creature on the earth. God, the just judge, will destroy the wicked, but He will also spare the innocent, and in His mercy He will permit the world to make a fresh start.

God's instructions to Noah on how to build the ark and what to take into the ark were detailed and precise. Recall that Adam received only one command from God, and he broke it; Noah, on the other hand, received a boatload of directions, yet he did everything exactly as God commanded. As a model of obedience and righteousness, he was the right man to repopulate the earth.

Even with the help of his three sons, Shem, Ham, and Japheth, it would take Noah decades to complete the ark. By the way, Genesis tells us that Noah did not have children until "after [he] was five hundred years old," and that the ark was finished "in the six hundredth year of Noah's life." We know that people married young in ancient times, so the three brothers were probably in their teens when they began work on the ark. It was an enormous job, but at least they had metal tools—saws, planes, nails, hammers—thanks to Tubalcain, Noah's brother or half-brother, who "was the forger of all instruments of bronze and iron." (Genesis 4.22) In other words, Uncle Tubalcain was the world's first blacksmith.

Metal saws notwithstanding, it was an enormous job finding the right sized trees, cutting them down, trimming off the branches, scraping off the bark, then cutting the trunks into planks and beams, and finally hauling the lumber back to the construction site. We can only hope that by the time Noah and his boys got busy, mankind had invented the wheel.

A WOODEN STONEHENGE

Noah and his family did not live on the seacoast. Maybe their home was beside a river—the Tigris or the Euphrates, perhaps. The family's mammoth construction project attracted the attention of the neighbors, naturally, and when they learned that Noah and his sons were building an enormous boat because utter destruction was coming upon the world in the form a flood, the neighborhood wits had a field day. The wisecracks and the raucous laughter angered Shem and hurt the feelings of Japeth, but they made Ham cringe. His friends were in the crowd, mocking him for being such a goof; he knew he would never have their respect again. The good opinion of these people mattered to Ham. He did not doubt his father's goodness, or that God had intervened to save Noah's family, but why must deliverance come at such a high price—the derision of his friends? Then it occurred to Ham that when the ark was finished, all the people making fun of him now would drown, and that thought made him feel much better.

Upright man that he was, Noah could not bear to think of all these people perishing. So, standing on a ladder propped against the side of the ark, and brandishing a hammer for emphasis, he urged the crowd to repent their sins, to return to the Lord; perhaps He would spare the world after all. Noah's appeals fell on deaf ears. But if the neighbors did not repent, at least in time they got bored with making fun of the boat-builders. Soon, no one came around the construction site anymore. And as the years passed the massive weight of the ark caused it settle into the earth like a wooden Stonehenge.

CLUELESS

The Apostle Peter tells us that in the time it took Noah to build the ark, "God's patience waited" (1 Peter 3.20) for the people of the world to clean up their act. But no one did. They went about their lives as usual, as Christ says in Luke's gospel. "They ate, they drank, they married, they were given in marriage, until the day when Noah entered the ark." (Luke 17.27) They went about their own lives, oblivious as ever to the things of God.

When the ark was complete, Noah and his family started rounding up the living creatures that would live on board with them. On

HAM: WHAT ARE YOU LOOKING AT?

the second and third decks, Noah and his sons had fashioned compartments and stalls for the animals. Food and fodder they would store on the first deck, where the family would have their quarters.

When Noah had accomplished everything God had commanded, God returned to give him a warning. "In seven days I will send rain upon the earth for forty days and forty nights; and every living thing that I have made I will blot out from the face of the ground."

After a busy week of loading the ark with the creatures, the supplies, and their bedding and personal possessions, Noah and his wife, and Shem, Ham, and Japeth and their wives, walked up the gangplank. The boys pulled it into the ark. Noah closed the heavy door in the side of the ark, and bolted it. The family climbed up to their quarters on the first deck where they sat down to wait.

THE DELUGE

Soon, it began to rain.

Actually, "began to rain" doesn't come close to what happened. The author of Genesis supplies a more vivid picture of the cataclysm. "All the fountains of the great deep burst forth, and the windows of the heavens were opened." The natural barriers which God set during the creation of the world to separate the waters from the dry land burst asunder, and as the rivers, lakes, and seas surged over the land, sheets of rain fell from the sky.

The panic of everyone outside the ark is inconceivable. How long did Noah and his family sit huddled in their quarters, listening to their neighbors pounding desperately on the ark door? Could they hear the cries of terror, or would the howling wind have drowned out all other sounds? Then came the frightening moment when the current and the rising water shook the ark loose from the ground into which it had settled. The violent rocking of the ark terrified everyone and everything inside the great ship, and animals and humans cried, and roared, and bleated in fear. They were safe from destruction, but not from the buffeting winds or the pounding waves.

With the great door bolted and the windows shut tight, Noah and his family could not see what was happening in the outside world. It was just as well. People drowned in their own homes, or were swept off their roofs. Violent waves splintered overcrowded ships and small boats, and ripped the sturdiest trees up by the roots, spilling into the dark water all the poor souls who had sought safety in the branches.

And there were the animals—shrieking and squealing in terror as they struggled to swim, then one by one sank beneath the waves. Most of "the creeping things" drowned in the first rush of the deluge, but the snakes lasted longer, roiling on the surface of the flood in huge venomous tangles, sinking their fangs into any human or beast that crashed into them, until finally the snakes sank, too. The birds held out a bit longer, but not much. Their wings were no match against the powerful winds; with no place to perch or seek shelter, they tumbled into the vast universal sea.

For forty days and forty nights the rains fell without ever easing up, until every mountain peak was submerged. Only when the deluge had scrubbed clean every inch of the earth did the rain stop. In that great and terrible flood, God "blotted out every living thing that was upon the face of the ground, man and animals and creeping things and birds of the air." Only Noah and his family and the creatures with him inside the ark remained alive. For 150 days Noah and his family tended the creatures in the ark, and waited. They were adrift on a vast ocean that covered even the highest mountain peaks, and although, bit by bit, the waters were receding, the Noah family did not notice. Until the day the ark bumped into something big. With a loud rasping sound, the ark ran aground on the summit of Mount Ararat in Armenia.

This was the family's first sign that the flood would dissipate, and they were euphoric. And after so many months rocking on the waves, it was a relief to be settled and stable again. More weeks of waiting lay ahead of them as the water ran back to its antediluvian limits in rivers and streams and oceans. And then the land had to dry out. They were all impatient—the animals, too—to get out of the boat, to escape the smells that were a natural by-product of having of all those animals on board. At last God told Noah, "Go forth from the ark."

Noah and sons swung back the large door in the side of the ark, and with the help of their wives began driving the living creatures down the gangplank and into the large empty world. Outside the ark, the earth was dry. Sprigs of small plants were breaking through the crust, so life was returning. But the world was deathly still—aside from the ark's passengers, there was nothing and no one left alive on the planet.

To give thanks for their deliverance, Noah built an altar and offered a sacrifice to God. As the fragrance of the sacrifice rose to heaven, God promised, "I will never again curse the ground because of man, for the imagination of man's heart is evil from his youth; neither will I ever again destroy every living creature as I have done. While the earth remains, seedtime and harvest, cold and heat, summer and winter, day and night, shall not cease."

To Noah and his family, God repeated the command he had first given to Adam and Eve: "Be fruitful and multiply and fill the earth." Then God said to Noah and his family, "This is the sign of the covenant I make between me and you and every living creature that is with you, for all future generations: I set my bow in the cloud, and it shall be a sign of the covenant between me and the earth."

THE WORLD'S FIRST HANGOVER

Rebuilding civilization kept the Noah family very busy, but in their spare time Ham and his wife had a son whom they named Canaan. The world was on its way to being peopled again—one baby at a time.

Noah also took a break from the labor of building and farming. He planted a vineyard, and when the grapes were ripe he made wine. And when the wine was fermented, he poured himself a cup. It wasn't bad. So he poured himself a second cup, which tasted even better. One cup led to another and then to another until Noah was thoroughly, completely soused. Now it seemed to him that he needed a nap, so he staggered back to his tent, threw off all his clothes, and passed out on the floor.

He was too old to carry on like this; a man over 600 years old should know when he's had enough; no wonder Ham laughed when he saw Noah sprawled out on the floor naked.

While Noah was in this undignified condition, Ham walked into the tent. He thought the sight of father, over 600 years old, buck naked and out cold, was hilarious. So he went outside to bring in Shem and Japeth so they could see how ridiculous the old man looked. Shem and Japeth didn't think their father's condition was especially funny; and given Noah's very advanced age, seeing him naked would not exactly be an aesthetic experience. So the boys took a voluminous robe and, placing it over their shoulders, walked backwards into the tent. When they had gotten to the point where they could see their father's feet, they averted their faces, and covered Noah up.

Ham thought his brothers' hypersensitivity was almost as funny as their father's boozing.

The next day Noah came to. His mouth was dry and felt strangely furry. His stomach was churning. His head felt like someone was splitting it open with a chisel. Sitting upright was difficult; standing upright was just not gonna happen. Worst of all was having to endure a lecture from his wife: He was too old to carry on

HAM: WHAT ARE YOU LOOKING AT?

like this; a man over 600 years old should know when he's had enough; no wonder Ham laughed when he saw Noah sprawled out on the floor naked.

That last part got Noah's attention, and his wife realized she should have kept that detail to herself. Lousy as Noah felt, he insisted on hearing the whole story, and the more he heard, the angrier he became. Bad enough that Ham had found his father in such a shameful condition, but instead of doing the decent thing—covering Noah and keeping the incident to himself—Ham had mocked his father, and called in his brothers so they could share the joke, too.

Hungover, humiliated, and angry, Noah lashed out at Ham, cursing him and even Ham's son, Canaan. But Shem and Japeth he blessed.

WHAT HAM
can teach us

THE COVENANT WITH NOAH IS AN ACT OF GOD'S GRACE, FREELY GIVEN

On the day Noah and his family left the ark, God made them a promise—that he would never wipe out all living things again. He required nothing from Noah or his descendants; God just made the promise. Like creation itself, this covenant is a sign of God's love. There is nothing humankind did to deserve it, or could do to deserve it; God simply wills it to be so. And he pours out his grace on humankind so we will be able to recognize this marvelous thing, and receive it with gratitude and joy.

"For I delight in the law of God in my inmost self." (Romans 7:22)

GO EASY ON THE BOOZE

The ancient Greeks had a saying, "Everything in moderation." That includes wine. And chocolate. And you want to keep an eye on the carbs. They are all good things, but they can be abused. Many people avoid alcohol altogether—it has injured so many families and destroyed so many lives. If you feel you have the tendency to overindulge or abuse alcohol, take a look at your habits and their effect on you and others, and get help if you need it.

"Thou dost cause the grass to grow for the cattle, and plants for man to cultivate, that he may bring forth food from the earth, and wine to gladden the heart of man." (Psalm 104:14–15)

MODESTY IS STILL A VIRTUE

These days, well-toned bodies are used to sell everything from gym memberships to soft drinks. But modesty—how we appear and how we look at others—is a valuable virtue to reclaim. All those almost-naked bodies in advertisements, in movies, on TV, can reduce those individuals, those children of God, into simply good-looking objects. And we who do the ogling—we run the risk of becoming voyeurs. We don't always have to take the bait—that's our choice.

"Blessed are the pure in heart, for they shall see God." (Matthew 5:8)

HONOR AND RESPECT YOUR PARENTS

The father of a family stands in the place of God the Father. The requirement to respect the father—and the mother—does not end once the kid becomes an adult and moves out of the house. And that respect is rooted in gratitude: After all, it was Mom and Dad who brought us into the world, and by their love and hard work showed us how to be faithful children of the Lord and productive members of society. Even when our parents' actions are somewhat less than perfect, we owe them the respect due them as our elders and as those who gave us life.

"And he went down with them and came to Nazareth,
and was obedient to them; and his mother kept all these things
in her heart. And Jesus increased in wisdom and in stature,
and in favor with God and man." (Luke 2:51–52)

CHOOSE THE RIGHT PATH

Ham had to know what he was doing was flat-out wrong. He had been brought up in a Godly family. Because of their faithfulness, the whole family had been spared when the rest of the world was wiped clean by the flood. When he found his father in that shameful condition, Ham had a choice: to cover Noah, and walk away, or to exploit his father's degradation for his own amusement. His conscience told Ham which was the right choice, but he ignored it.

"Blessed is the man who walks not in the counsel of the wicked,
nor stands in the way of sinners, nor sits in the seat of scoffers;
but his delight is the law of the Lord." (Psalm 1:1–2)

CHAPTER 3

LOT'S DAUGHTERS

THE MOST BADDEST
GIRLS OF THE BIBLE

Genesis 19

What are two marriageable daughters to do? Their home—Sodom and nearby Gomorrah—destroyed by God's wrath, their fiancés killed in the commotion and their mother turned into a pillar of salt, and the girls and their father banished from the town where they sought refuge. The future did not look bright. Instead of trusting in God, however, they turned to their father, Lot, for answers—but not in a way that any child ever should.

In the catalog of bad girls of the Bible, when it comes to sheer breathtaking wickedness it's hard to beat the daughters of Lot. The author of Genesis does not even tell us their names; considering the awfulness of their sin, better they should remain anonymous.

Lot was Abraham's nephew, and their two clans had lived as one. But as both men prospered, their combined flocks and herds became too large for the land of Canaan to support them. For their mutual benefit the two men decided to separate, and Abraham, ever the generous uncle, urged Lot to decide what he preferred to do—to remain in Canaan, or to settle elsewhere. After scouting the territory, Lot "saw the Jordan valley was well watered everywhere like the garden of the Lord" (Genesis 13:10), so he chose to relocate there, near the cities of Sodom and Gomorrah, and the little town of Zoar. Genesis also mentions, a few lines later, "Now the men of Sodom were wicked, great sinners against the Lord." Apparently neither Lot nor Abraham was aware of the town's unsavory reputation.

UNCORRUPTED AND FAITHFUL

While Abraham continued his nomadic lifestyle, living in his tent and moving his flocks and herds from one green pasture to the next, Lot moved into Sodom, married, and had two daughters. Like Noah and his family, Lot and his family remained uncorrupted by their neighbors and faithful to God. As for everyone else in Sodom and Gomorrah, it appears that they got worse and worse—so bad, in fact, that the Lord came down from heaven with two angels to settle matters.

On His way to the two cities, the Lord and the angels stopped to visit with Abraham and assure him that in a year's time Sarah would at last give birth to the son they had longed for. Then followed the most famous conversation in the Old Testament as Abraham bargained with the Lord, urging Him to agree not to destroy Sodom if a certain number of righteous people could be found in the city—first 50, then 45, then 40, then 30, then 20, and finally ten. "For the sake of ten I will not destroy it," the Lord promised. But when his angels arrived in Sodom, they found no more than six who deserved to be saved—Lot, his wife, his two daughters, and the girls' fiancés. Alas, the prospective bridegrooms refused to leave the doomed city, and the number of God-fearing people in Sodom dropped to a mere four.

By this time Lot had a pretty good idea of what his neighbors were capable of, because when he spotted the strangers—the angels in human form—approaching Sodom, he invited them to spend the night at his house. Such courtesy to strangers was standard, even a sacred duty, in the ancient world, and examples can be found in all societies of the Middle East and around the Mediterranean. But when the angels replied, "No; we will spend the night in the street," Lot shifted from courteous to insistent; "he urged them strongly" not to camp out in Sodom. And so the angels entered Lot's home, where they were welcomed and fed.

After dinner, just as the family and their guests were preparing to go to sleep, every man and every teenage boy in Sodom gathered outside Lot's house. "Where are the men who came to you tonight?" they shouted to Lot. "Bring them out to us that we may know them."

There is some discussion these days about what the men of Sodom had in mind. The rest of the scene outside Lot's house makes it clear that when the men and boys of Sodom expressed an interest in "knowing" the strangers, they meant it in the traditional biblical sense of sexual relations. Stepping outside his door, Lot appealed to his neighbors. "I beg you, my brothers, do not act so wickedly. Behold, I have two daughters who have not known man; let me bring them out to you, and do to them as you please; only do nothing to these men, for they have come under the shelter of my roof."

Lot's offer makes it clear that he understood the mob in front of his house were using the phrase "know them" in the sexual sense. Lot used the word "know" it the same way when he tried to buy off the mob with his daughters "who have not known man" (clearly, they were virgins). But the men and teenage boys of Sodom would not be put off. As they closed in on Lot, the angels reached outside, pulled their host inside, shut the door, then struck every member of the mob blind.

THE FLIGHT FROM SODOM

The next morning the angels collected the little band of refugees and, taking them by the hands, hustled them out of doomed Sodom. "Flee for your life," the angels commanded, "do not look back or stop anywhere in the valley; flee to the hills lest you be consumed."

Lot was in a state of panic. He dreaded fleeing into the wilderness. Like his uncle Abraham, he tried to negotiate a better deal with the angels, and all these thousands of years later we can still hear the desperation in his voice.

"Behold, yonder city is near enough to flee to," he said, "and it is a small one. Let me escape there—is it not a small one?—and my life will be saved!" Out of compassion for this frightened family, one of the angels granted this favor, even promising not to rain down destruction on Sodom and Gomorrah until the refugees were safely inside the gates of the nearby town of Zoar. As Lot and his family ran toward Zoar, they could hear a howling wind followed by a dreadful roar, and they felt on their backs the terrible heat of an immense conflagration.

So it must have been at the town gate, at the very threshold of safety, that Lot's wife let her curiosity get the best of her; disregarding the angels' earlier warning, she stopped and turned to look at the destruction that pursued them. And at that moment she was turned into a pillar of salt. With this fresh grief weighing down his heart, Lot hurried on into Zoar.

Lot did not find a warm welcome in Zoar. The presence of the sole survivors of the utter destruction of Sodom and Gomorrah made the Zoarites worry that Lot and his daughters might be lightning rods who would draw down the wrath of the Lord on their town. And who could blame them? From miles off Abraham—and all the townsfolk—saw the billowing cloud of smoke that signaled the destruction of the two cities; when the fire and brimstone fell from heaven, the people of Zoar had front-row seats.

Afraid to remain in Zoar, Lot took his daughters and did as the angels had advised in the first place—he went into the hills. They found a large cave, and made their new home inside it.

FAMILY LIFE IN THE CAVE

At least since the fifth or sixth century A.D., a cave overlooking the Dead Sea has been identified as Lot's Cave. Christians erected a church adjacent to it, and for many years pilgrims came to pray at the site. Perhaps there was a longstanding oral tradition in the region that this cave was Lot's last home, or perhaps devout Christians came to the conclusion that this cave, near as it is to the valley where Sodom and Gomorrah once stood, must have been the one in which Lot lived with his daughters.

With their prospective bridegrooms among the casualties of Sodom and the men of Zoar showing no signs of interest in them, Lot's daughters came to the conclusion that no man would ever want to marry them. But they still wanted children. What to do? The eldest girl had an idea. "Come," she said to her sister, "let us make our father drink wine, and we will lie with him, that we may preserve offspring through our father." As incredible as it may sound, this struck the younger sister as a good idea.

That night the daughters plied poor, unsuspecting Lot with so much wine that when his first-born daughter climbed into bed with him, "he did not know when she lay down or when she arose." And on the next night, it was the younger daughter's turn. By this vile trick the daughters of Lot became pregnant. Both gave birth to sons, Moab and Benammi, who became the founders of the Moabites and the Ammonites, both of whom would give the Israelites trouble later.

Strange to say, there are people in Jordan today who pride themselves on being descended from Lot. They tend not to mention his daughters—call it "selective memory."

WHAT LOT'S DAUGHTERS
can teach us

GOD IS EXTREMELY PATIENT

In Shakespeare's play *The Merchant of Venice*, Portia says, "In the course of justice, none of us should see salvation." Ain't that the truth. All of us fall so short of the mark it is a wonder that the angels don't have Heaven all to themselves. How long did God wait for the people of Sodom and Gomorrah to turn away from their wickedness and return to him? Years, certainly, perhaps even centuries. And the Lord is equally patient with us, waiting day after day, year after year, for us to give up our sins and failings. Pray then for mercy, and do not fail to extend mercy to your neighbors.

"The Lord is merciful and gracious, slow to anger and abounding in steadfast love." (Psalm 103:8)

THE WRATH OF GOD IS NOT INDISCRIMINATE

When Abraham interceded for those inhabitants of Sodom and Gomorrah who were innocent, he asked God, "Wilt thou indeed destroy the righteous with the wicked?... Shall not the Judge of all the earth do right?" (Genesis 18:23, 25) The answer is that God the righteous Judge will not lash out and destroy the innocent along with the wicked. That is why He saved Noah and his family, and Lot and his family, and was even willing to spare Lot's future sons-in-law if only they'd had the good sense to get out of the city. God is the ultimate Just Judge, who tempers His justice with mercy.

"Wisdom rescued from troubles those who served her." (Wisdom 10:9)

PERSEVERE IN YOUR GOOD INTENTIONS AND BELIEF IN GOD

Many Christians think that if they could only see a great miracle, just once, they would remain faithful to God forever. Surely, they would be so inspired by His power that they'd easily be able to practice virtue and avoid sin.

If only that were true! It just doesn't seem to work that way for us humans. Shortly after the Israelites saw God part the Red Sea, they were worshipping an idol of a golden calf; just weeks after he saw Christ raise Lazarus from the dead, Judas betrayed the Lord for thirty pieces of silver. Lot's wife is simply one more example of someone who has experienced direct divine intervention in her life, but instead of remaining steadfast in her trust, she let idle curiosity get the better of her. In our own lives, do we honor God's interventions and answers to our troubles in ways that speak to our faith?

"I have set before you life and death, blessing and curse; therefore choose life, that you and your descendants may live, loving the Lord your God, obeying his voice, and cleaving to him." (Deuteronomy 30:19–20)

SIN CAN BE CONTAGIOUS

Lot should have thought twice about settling his family in so infamous a city as Sodom. It may have been comfortable and good for business, but it gave his daughters such a bad example that when they were alone and there was no one around to show them a better way, they committed the terrible sin of incest with their father.

All of us, children and adults, are susceptible to unwholesome influences. We hope that our own beliefs and teachings to our children can see us through such exposures, leading us to choose the right path. But even the strongest and best-intentioned person can succumb to bad influences. It does seem wise to limit exposure to what we can, saving our strength for bigger tests.

"You shall not follow a multitude to do evil." (Exodus 23:2)

44

TRUST IN GOD'S PLAN

When Lot's daughters despaired of ever finding husbands and starting families of their own, their answer to their dilemma was to hatch a truly evil scheme. We are left to wonder why they didn't turn to God for help and answers. After all, He had just sent angels to save them from utter destruction. Is it so unlikely that He would not have helped them find husbands?

Genesis never tells us that the girls prayed for divine assistance. Instead, they hatched a disgusting scheme to become mothers, a scheme that defiled their father and sullied their reputations forever. It does make you ask what God's plan for their lives might have been—and how different things might have been had they trusted Him.

"Our God whom we serve is able to deliver us out of the burning fiery furnace." (Daniel 3:17)

"She said to herself, 'If I only touch his garment, I shall be made well.'" (Matthew 9:21)

CHAPTER 4

JACOB

DOUBLE TROUBLE

Genesis 25:21–34, 27:1–45

When a parent favors one child over another—and has no problem expressing that preference to anyone who will listen—that's a lesson in bad parenting. Sometimes, the resentment such conduct causes can shift into overdrive, as it did for Jacob, who was jealous of his first-born twin brother, Esau. Fueled by his cunning mother, Rebecca, Jacob committed a shameful act that destroyed the family and brought unmitigated grief to his dying father.

Brothers will fight. It's as inevitable as death and taxes. But Jacob and Esau started brawling while they were in their mother's womb. Rebecca, who had been slow to conceive, didn't know if she could stand it—this was worse than any pregnancy horror story she'd ever heard. "Why do I live?" she asked herself, and since she couldn't think of a satisfactory answer, she took her problem to the Lord.

"Two nations are in your womb," the Lord said, "and two peoples, born of you, shall be divided; the one shall be stronger than the other."

Well, that explained things at least.

BATTLING BABIES

On the day Rebecca went into labor, the twins inside her were still fighting—this time to see who would be the first one out. The biggest twin, a ruddy skinned, robust little guy, arrived first, but his little brother hadn't given up—he entered the world with one hand clutching the first-born's heel. Rebecca and Isaac named their first-born Esau; the second-born they named Jacob.

As the boys grew, Esau proved to be the outgoing, physical type. He liked roughhousing in the fields, he had the men in the tribe teach him to hunt. Jacob, on the other hand, was a quiet kid, a homebody, happy to hang around the tent. Isaac, who had a taste for wild game, favored Esau the hunter. Rebecca, who liked having one of her boys around her, favored the mild-mannered Jacob.

In ancient times, being the first-born son was a big deal. Just as the first fruits of the harvest and the first youngling among the livestock were sacred to God and offered as a sacrifice to the Lord, the first-born was also sacred. Instead of being sacrificed, though, the first-born son enjoyed a host of privileges. He was the future head of the family; he carried on the family line; at his father's death, when the estate was divided up among the children, the first born was entitled to at least a double share, or more if his father had made such a stipulation. There were only three ways a younger son could assume the rights of the first-born: through the death the eldest, through his disinheritance, or by purchasing the eldest's birthright.

LIFE-LONG RIVALS

Child psychologists have observed that in general, sister/sister twins tend to be very close, while brother/brother twins tend to be very competitive. Early on, Jacob had learned that in a fight, he could not beat Esau—the kid was too big and too strong. The only way to defeat his older brother was to outsmart him. So, while Esau was in the fields developing his muscles, Jacob sat at home pumping up his cunning.

According to the psychologists, around the time children are three years old, they've already mastered the fundamental rules of the house, and have figured out a few ways to manipulate them for their own benefit. In the years that follow, a child learns to compare and contrast his own position in the family with that of his brother or sister. And the little darling's radar is acutely sensitive to who is getting a tad more attention, or a smidgen more latitude. Esau noticed that Rebecca favored Jacob; Jacob noticed that Isaac favored Esau.

It started early, with Isaac bragging because Esau walked first, and Rebecca telling all the neighbors that Jacob spoke in complete sentences while his brother was still babbling baby-talk. It's a recipe for lifelong rivalry: You just know that in years to come the brothers would compete over who lived in the biggest tent, who had the largest flock of goats, who rode the nicest camel.

In many families it is commonplace for resentment to erupt into total war. In the tent of Isaac and Rebecca, however, sibling rivalry simmered just below the surface, as Jacob watched for opportunities to take advantage of Esau. Jacob's patience would be rewarded.

THE ART OF THE DEAL

It was a beautiful, crisp autumn day. Esau had risen early to go hunting; Jacob had remained at home where he cooked up a tasty batch of lentil soup. Around midday Esau returned and made a beeline for the cooking fire where Jacob sat tasting his soup and adjusting the seasoning.

"Let me eat some of that red pottage," Esau said, "for I am famished!"

Jacob put down the ladle, looked up at his brother with an expression of pure innocence upon his face, and replied, "First sell me your birthright."

Incredibly, there is an ancient Mesopotamian tablet that has come down to us which records a similar event. According to the inscription on the tablet, Tupkitilla, the first-born son of his family, found himself in certain difficulties. Because of that, he agreed to sell his birthright to his younger brother, Kurpazah, in exchange for three sheep.

Tupkitilla was better at the art of the deal than Esau who, when presented with the choice between a bowl of soup and the rights and privileges that were his as the first-born son, renounced his birthright and took the soup.

But Jacob didn't hand his brother that bowl of lentil soup yet; he wanted a little something more from Esau. "Swear to me first," Jacob demanded. And so Esau swore that he agreed to resign his birthright to Jacob in exchange for a bowl of soup.

In a society where almost no one could read or write, such oral agreements, backed up by a solemn oath, were universally recognized as legally binding. Jacob had just acquired all the rights and privileges of the first-born, something he had wanted since he and his brother were duking it out inside their poor mother's womb. And now that he had the birthright, Jacob became magnanimous—in addition to the soup, he gave Esau some bread, too.

MOTHER AND CHILD

Acquiring Esau's birthright was a coup, but Jacob wanted one more thing: He also wanted their father's final blessing. This would be trickier to get than the birthright. For the rest of his days, Isaac never forgot how Jacob bamboozled Esau; he was determined to make what amends he could by bestowing his final blessing on his beloved Esau.

51

The years passed and Isaac's death drew near. From his deathbed, Isaac, now blind, called for Esau. "Behold, I am old," Isaac said, "I do not know the day of my death. Now then, take your weapons, your quiver and your bow, and go out to the field, and hunt game for me, and prepare for me savory food, such as I love, and bring it to me that I may eat; that I may bless you before I die."

And so off into the field went Esau, a dutiful son and a hunter without guile.

Now, Rebecca had been eavesdropping at the tent flap when Isaac spoke with Esau. Once her elder boy was gone, she called her darling Jacob to her. The first time he cheated Esau, Jacob had worked alone; this time his mother would team up with him. She sent him to the flock with orders to kill two good kids, which she would cook in the savory style so that Isaac would mistake the kid meat for wild game. "You shall bring it to your father to eat," she told Jacob, "so he may bless you before he dies."

But Jacob spotted one flaw in his mother's scheme. Esau, that walking dynamo of testosterone, had a thick pelt of hair on his chest and arms and legs, while Jacob was as smooth as a girl. If Isaac's hand brushed against Jacob, he would know by touch that this was not Esau, that Jacob was trying to scam him. "I shall seem to be mocking him," Jacob said, "and bring a curse upon myself, not a blessing."

Rebecca had already thought of that, but she hadn't time to explain at that moment. She shooed Jacob out of the tent and off to the flock, while she started her prep work at the kitchen fire.

While the kid meat cooked, Rebecca took the goatskins and covered Jacob's neck and forearms with them. Then she ladled the savory stew into a bowl, handed it to Jacob, and pushed him through the tent flap to his dying father's side.

ONE LAST SCAM

Tripping, almost spilling the stew, Jacob stumbled into his father's room. Then, recovering his poise as well as his balance, he called out, "My father!"

Isaac could not see, of course, so he asked a natural question, "Who are you my son?"

Jacob, smooth as ever, replied, "I am Esau your first-born. I have done as you told me; now sit up and eat of my game, that you may bless me." But mentioning the blessing up front had been a mistake. Jacob has rushed things, and it made Isaac suspicious.

"How is it that you have found it so quickly, my son?" he asked.

Shameless liar that he was, Jacob replied, "Because the Lord your God granted me success."

But Isaac was not convinced. "Come near, that I may feel you, my son, to know whether you are really my son Esau or not."

Jacob's heart was pounding in his chest, but he had gone too far to lose courage now. He approached his father, and let the old man run his hands over him. The goatskins fooled Isaac. "The voice is Jacob's voice," he said, "but the hands are the hands of Esau." Poor Isaac—he was no match for a conspiracy between Rebecca and Jacob.

After he had finished his meal, Isaac called for Jacob to come close once again, and now he pronounced the final blessing in which he prayed that God would shower this boy with prosperity and power over his enemies. The sentence Jacob and Rebecca were waiting for— she was eavesdropping at the tent flap again—came at the end. "Be lord over your brothers, and may your mother's sons bow down to you. Cursed be every one who curses you, and blessed be every one who blesses you!"

Jacob did not hang around to make conversation. The blessing done, he rose and scurried out of the tent—and not a moment too soon. Esau arrived soon thereafter, the scent of the fields still clinging to his clothes, his face glowing from the exertion of the hunt, and in

JACOB: DOUBLE TROUBLE

his hands a steaming bowl of game he had prepared himself for Isaac. Happy, confident, brimming with expectation, Esau said, "Let my father arise, and eat of his son's game, that you may bless me."

Filled with consternation, Isaac asked a question to which he already knew the answer, "Who are you?"

Esau, not suspecting a thing, answers, "I am your son, your first-born, Esau."

The blind old man, trembling with rage at having been deceived by his own child, asked another question to which he and Esau already knew the answer. "Who was it then that hunted game and brought it to me, and I ate it all before you came, and I have blessed him? Yes, and he shall be blessed."

That final statement, "Yes, and he shall be blessed," was Isaac's assertion that like Esau's formal oath a few years earlier, a deathbed blessing was final and irrevocable. No wonder Esau's response was to cry out "with an exceedingly great and bitter cry." Once again his brother had robbed him. Storming out of his father's tent in a terrible rage, Esau promised one of the members of the tribe, "The days of mourning for my father are approaching; then I will kill my brother Jacob."

Rebecca, who had a talent for hearing everything that went on in her household, learned of Esau's promise to murder Jacob; she knew her first-born son well enough to be afraid. Esau was strong, he could be violent, he knew how to use weapons, and he had every reason to kill his deceptive little brother. There was at least one bit of good news—Esau didn't know the part his mother had played in the conspiracy to cheat him out of his father's blessing. And so Rebecca made a suggestion to Jacob that he should go visit her brother, his Uncle Laban, for a while—just until Esau had calmed down. Smart boy that he was, Jacob didn't have to be told twice. He cleared out that same day.

It would be twenty years before the brothers saw one another again, and when they did, Jacob would not be at all eager to meet Esau face-to-face.

WHAT JACOB
can teach us

PEACE ON EARTH BEGINS AT HOME

The world is a violent place, full of hatred and conflict. But what good is yearning for world peace if scarcely a week goes by when we do not go nine rounds with some member of our family? Charity, respect, forbearance, patience. If we can't exercise these virtues with the people who are nearest and dearest to us, what are the odds that we—or anyone else—will practice them on strangers?

Have your interactions with family brought joy and harmony, or have they created tension and misunderstanding? If you can create a loving and peaceful environment at home, odds are you'll carry that message into the world outside your doors.

"Behold, how good and pleasant it is when brothers dwell in unity!"
(Psalm 133:1) "Strive for peace with all men, and for holiness without
which no one will see the Lord." (Hebrews 12:14)

UNDERSTAND WHAT TRULY MOTIVATES YOUR ACTIONS

Any one of us can be very gifted at rationalizing our actions, fully capable of justifying or excusing a deed that's borderline acceptable—or just plain rotten. We may be able to fool other people, but in our hearts, we know the truth about our motivations.

Of course, there is no way to hide our motives from the eyes of God. Jacob and Rebecca thought they were terribly clever, but to achieve their purpose they did irreparable harm to their own family. How do you suppose they attempted to justify their actions to God?

"Every way of a man is right in his own eyes, but the Lord weighs the heart." (Proverbs 21:2)

"O Lord, thou hast searched me and known me . . . thou discernest my thoughts from afar." (Psalm 139:1–2)

"We must not put the Lord to the test." (1 Corinthians 10:9)

THERE'S A REASON WHY ENVY IS ONE OF THE SEVEN DEADLY SINS

The great fourth-century theologian Augustine believed that the devil tempted Adam and Eve out of envy: He hated seeing them blissfully happy in Eden while he was gnashing his teeth with his fellow devils in Hell. Jacob signed on to the devil's party when he schemed to bring down Esau and take what belonged rightfully to his brother. Jacob compounded his sin by taking pleasure in scamming Esau, not to mention his blind, dying father.

The antidote to envy is to congratulate your brother or sister who is enjoying success. Emulate those qualities in them that you admire, and understand your own special gifts and blessings. In someone else's eyes, you may be the model of success.

"Through the devil's envy death entered the world, and those who belong to his party experience it." (Wisdom 2:24)

WINNING ISN'T EVERYTHING

The world values success. The underdog who comes from behind and wins big will always be a favorite cover story on business and investment magazines. The question is, "How was that success achieved?" Unfair business practices, exploitation of workers, flat-out lying and cheating will elicit cries of admiration in certain quarters. You don't want to spend any time in those types of quarters. Jacob wanted the rights of the first-born, and he did not care what he had to do to get them. In the end, he was willing to trample over his own brother and father to get what he wanted.

Always ask: Is the price worth the reward? Then ask: What is my measure of success? If it's gained at someone else's expense, reevaluate your yardstick.

"And what does the Lord require of you but to do justice, and to love kindness, and to walk humbly with your God?" (Micah 6:8)

"Do not be conformed to this world but be transformed by the renewal of your mind, that you may prove what is the will of God, what is good and acceptable and perfect." (Romans 12:2)

THE RESPECT DUE TO PARENTS AND MEMBERS OF OUR FAMILY IS A SACRED TRUST

The source and model of the human family is God the Father. There is no difference between the love and reverence we owe to God as his children, and the love and respect we owe to our fathers and mothers. Even in families that are dysfunctional beyond repair, there are still bonds of obligation.

In his all-out, no-holds-barred, take-no-prisoners approach to getting what did not belong to him, Jacob jettisoned the respect he owed to his father, Isaac. To help him achieve it, Rebecca jettisoned the respect she owed to her husband and to her son Esau. We can only imagine how tense and uncomfortable life was in the family tent after Jacob ran away to his Uncle Laban. After so many years of marriage, Rebecca had lost the trust of her dying husband. Isaac. And can you imagine what disappointment and grief must have clouded the last moments Isaac and Esau shared?

In our own words and actions with our parents and our siblings, it's wise to remember that we are always building a framework that supports our family structure. Is yours a solid framework that you can be proud of?

"With all your heart, honor your father, and do not forget the birth pangs of your mother. Remember that through your parents you were born; and what can you give back to them that equals their gift to you?" (Sirach 7:27–28)

CHAPTER 5

THE TEN ELDEST SONS OF JACOB

THE MOB MENTALITY

Genesis 34: 1–31; 35:1

We've all seen it happen. People who, individually, are perfectly nice and reasonable can get drawn into an unruly mob, intent on revenge; reason and lawfulness go right out the window. Is that what happened in the case of Dinah and her brothers, Jacob's sons? Dinah had been assaulted, and although things were being settled between the families according to the laws of the time, the boys just couldn't let it be. In their arrogance, they took a painful, bad situation . . . and made it much, much worse.

The older kids get, the more problems they can cause their parents, and the ten eldest sons of Jacob were nonstop troublemakers. It may have been because there were so many of them—with all ten hanging around together all the time, they developed their own private mob mentality or herd behavior. Maybe the latter is a better term in this case; the boys did watch the livestock.

In herd behavior, a group, a crowd, or a mob take their cue from a few individuals who have rank or status. Watch a group of kids on the playground: You'll spot the leaders right away—they are the ones choosing the games, making the rules, and keeping the rest of the kids in line. (And it is distressing how often other kids will fall into line, even if the leader is a bossy little brat.)

On the playground, herd behavior is often just a childhood phase the kids will grow out of, but in rare and unfortunate cases, it lays the foundation for future gang behavior. Alas, the ten sons of Jacob did not grow out of this phase. If there were gangs in ancient Canaan, this one would have been known as "The Killer Shepherds."

As with all gangs, there was a hierarchy among the sons of Jacob. The older sons set the rules. In a society where a first-born son held all the cards, there was a lot of social pressure on the younger sons to defer to their older brother. Or brothers. And since the older boys were bigger and stronger than the younger boys, they enforced their authority in the way older brothers always have—by beating up unruly, disrespectful younger brothers. The ten sons of Jacob, then, were a cohesive unit, a bunch of bullies, and if something or someone set them off all hell broke loose.

PLAYING FAVORITES

At the risk of drifting into the Nature vs. Nurture debate, such bad behavior was probably not entirely 100 percent the boys' fault. They were all the sons either of Leah or of one of the two household slaves in Jacob's camp. You'll remember that Jacob worked seven years for his uncle Laban with the understanding that at the end of this period of indentured servitude Jacob would be permitted to marry Laban's lovely youngest daughter, Rachel. The seven years ended, everybody gathered for the wedding, and Laban presented Jacob with his daughter, heavily veiled according to the custom. Jacob's bride did not unveil herself until they had consummated the marriage—when to his shock poor Jacob found that he had been bamboozled, that Laban had pulled the old switcheroo. His new wife was not his beloved Rachel, but her older sister Leah. Jacob was stuck: The wedding ceremony had been witnessed, he had consummated the match, there was nothing he could do. But Laban wasn't entirely heartless; he assured Jacob that he could eventually marry Rachel—in exchange for another seven years of indentured servitude.

THE TEN ELDEST SONS OF JACOB: THE MOB MENTALITY

Once he had completed all those years of forced labor for Laban, Jacob took his wives and growing family and set out to establish his own household. And the Lord blessed Jacob with many children, abundant flocks and herds, and sufficient wealth that he could afford to purchase slaves. Yet in spite of all these blessings, there was tension in Jacob's family.

Everyone in Jacob's camp knew that Rachel was the patriarch's favorite wife, that in terms of affection, Leah came in a distant second. There is no record that Jacob mistreated Leah; he just didn't love her. He made love to her—all those sons were proof of that. He made love to two of his slaves, too—some of his sons were the children of these women (although by the custom of the times, these children were considered free, not slaves). It was galling to the boys that their father was barely more than civil to their mothers, and it made them feel that he barely loved them. In those days, a woman who gave her husband sons deserved respect, yet Jacob, in spite of the *ten sons* to whom Leah and the slave women had given birth, showed few signs of esteem or gratitude. This situation would only get worse when Rachel at long last did give birth to sons, Joseph and Benjamin, both of whom became Jacob's instant favorites. But we are getting ahead of ourselves—there is another chapter about Joseph.

It is a truth universally acknowledged, as Jane Austen would say, that parents who display favoritism among the children are unleashing a world of trouble in the home. From a young age children are sensitive to issues of fairness. How many play dates are punctuated by cries of, "That's not fair!" Granted, sometimes a kid's appeal to justice is a smoke screen for, "Give me what I want . . . now!" Nonetheless, if there is a consistent pattern of one child being pampered, petted, and indulged, the less-favored child or children will notice. First, they are hurt. Then, they are angry. And as the years roll by, anger turns into deep-seated resentment. In adulthood, the overlooked children of Jacob were seething with anger and resentment, ready to erupt in unexpected ways that would shock their clueless parents.

THE RAPE OF DINAH

Genesis tells us that Jacob had twelve sons and one daughter, Dinah, the daughter of Jacob's first wife, Leah. (Reading between the lines, it seems likely that there were other daughters, too, but Dinah is the only one we know by name.) Living in Jacob's family tent must have been like living in a locker room—the testosterone level was off the charts. To escape an environment dominated by boys whose favorite activities were brawling, belching, and scratching themselves, teenage Dinah looked beyond the camp for girlfriends.

The family had settled in the land of the Hivites, one of the pagan nations of Canaan about whom we know only a little. While Jacob and his clan were seminomads, dwelling in tents, the Hivites had a town as well as farms. Genesis tells us that Dinah liked to go "out to visit the women of the land." She made these visits around the countryside alone, without an escort or chaperone.

She had just spent a day with her Hivite girlfriends and was returning to her father's camp when Shechem, the Hivite prince, saw Dinah. He hurried to catch up with her. All his young life Shechem knew he enjoyed important advantages. At this point he, like Dinah, was in his teens. He was handsome, he was well-dressed, he was a prince of the land who one day would be king. Shechem was the walking, breathing fulfillment of a fairy tale. Dinah noticed Shechem's superficial charms, but she wasn't stupid: She was a girl alone with a strange boy, a situation about which her mother, Leah, had often warned her. She kept her side of the conversation to the bare minimum—polite, but reserved. She walked a little faster, but the prince kept pace with her. The boy could not take a hint, and he would not go away! Dinah promised herself the next time she visited her Hivite friends, she would have one of her father's slaves accompany her.

Shechem was dazzled by Dinah. She was beautiful, he was overcome with lust, and they were both alone. He grabbed her by both

THE TEN ELDEST SONS OF JACOB: THE MOB MENTALITY

wrists and dragged her off the path, to a clump of bushes, where he pinned Dinah to the ground. She fought, but he was too strong for her. She screamed, but he felt not a touch of shame or pity. She called for help, but there was no one to hear her. "He seized her and lay with her and humbled her," is the way the author of Genesis describes Shechem's rape of Dinah.

When he was done, Shechem had a change of heart. "His soul was drawn to Dinah," Genesis tells us, "he loved the maiden and spoke tenderly to her." Frightened, sick, and confused by the sudden change in the boy who had just assaulted her, Dinah wrapped her torn clothes around herself and ran for home. Sobbing, she told her horrified mother and father what Shechem had done to her. Her brothers, by the way, were not at home; they were in the fields with the herds.

Meanwhile, Shechem had also gone home where he admitted to his father, King Hamor, that he had forced himself on Dinah, the daughter of Jacob, and now he found himself hopelessly in love with the girl. "Get me this maiden for my wife," he begged his father.

STRIKING A DEAL

Well into the nineteenth century, even in the United States, there was a widespread belief that a woman who had been seduced or raped was dishonored and the only recourse was to compel the seducer or rapist to restore her reputation by marrying her. Today, such a notion is repellant to us, especially the idea of making a marriage between a rapist and his victim. Yet from the point of view of Jacob, Leah, and King Hamor, that was the only option, which isn't to say that the two families were happy about the situation. Jacob and Leah wanted Dinah to marry a Hebrew, someone who would love and cherish her. As for Hamor, his son was entirely in the wrong and he had to find some way to appease the outrage of the Israelites. The one advantage the king had was that Shechem was contrite, in love, and eager to marry Dinah.

So Hamor, with Shechem in tow, went to Jacob's encampment, hoping to mollify a family torn between rage and sorrow. Hamor had barely begun to speak with Jacob when the ten boys arrived, fresh from the fields. When they learned that Dinah had been raped by the prince, they went wild, shouting for vengeance and threatening to kill Shechem on the spot. But Hamor remained calm. Furthermore, he made his appeal directly to Jacob (the wisest course of action—he would not have gotten far with the boys). "The soul of my son Shechem longs for your daughter," the king said. "I pray you, give her to him in marriage."

We know that after he assaulted Dinah, Shechem "spoke tenderly" to Dinah; let's hope an abject apology was included in those tender words. Whether Dinah forgave Shechem and whether she was willing to marry the prince is not recorded. In his conversation with Jacob, Hamor laid the emphasis on how great good could emerge from this terrible assault: Following the example of Dinah and Shechem, the Hivites and the Hebrews would intermarry; the Hebrews would be free to buy farms or homes or shops in the town, and settle down. They would no longer be two separate nations but a single people.

Then Prince Shechem joined the discussion, trying to appease Jacob and his ten angry sons. "Let me find favor in your eyes," he said, "and whatever you say to me I will give. Ask of me ever so much as marriage present and gift, and I will give according as you say to me; only give me the maiden to be my wife."

Before their father could answer, the boys set their price. "We cannot do this thing, to give our sister to one who is uncircumcised, for that would be a disgrace to us. Only on this condition will we consent to you: that you will become as we are and every male of you be circumcised." Only then would it be proper for Dinah to marry

65

Shechem, and only then would the Hebrew women consider marrying Hivite men.

To the king and the prince, it seemed like they were getting off easy. The Hebrews might have demanded gold, livestock, and land, but instead, they wanted the Hivite men to undergo a surgical procedure. Hamor and Shechem agreed at once. Back at their town they convinced the Hivite men that a united Hebrew/Hivite nation would be make them stronger and wealthier. In exchange for such advantages, what were a few days of physical discomfort?

While all this wheeling and dealing was going on, where was poor Dinah? She was the main subject of conversation, of course, but the author of Genesis does not record a single word she said up to this point, or even how she reacted after the rape when Shechem suddenly began to speak tenderly to her. Yet she is the one person whose voice we would like to hear.

THE TREACHERY
OF JACOB'S TEN SONS

Jacob sent his mohels—the men expert at performing circumcisions—to Hamor's town. Genesis tells us Shechem "did not delay to do the thing, because he had delight in Jacob's daughter." Immediately after the prince had undergone the procedure, he and Dinah were married, and she moved into the palace with him. Following the prince's example, and in keeping with the deal they had struck with the Hebrews, Hamor the king and every male Hivite were all circumcised.

But it was not a deal. It was a ruse. The sons of Jacob had no intention of giving their sister in marriage to a Hivite, not even to a Hivite prince. Three days after Shechem's and Dinah's wedding, when every Hivite man and boy was in terrible pain and incapacitated by circumcision, Simeon and Levi, the second and third eldest sons of Jacob, led their brothers into the Hivite town. With their swords drawn, they burst into the palace where they found Hamor and Shechem writhing in agony on their beds. Jacob's sons murdered the king and the prince, then they dragged Dinah away and sent her back to their father's tent. From the palace Jacob's sons fanned out across the town, killing every Hivite man and boy, ransacking every house and shop, rounding up all the livestock, and taking all the Hivite women and children as slaves.

The noise of the animals, the wails of the women and children, and the exultant shouts of his sons brought Jacob out of his tent. He stood amazed as sheep, goats, cattle, asses, and weeping captives went by in a great cloud of dust. Driving them on were his ten sons, wrapped in the looted finery and wearing the stolen jewelry of the Hivites, their bloodstained swords still in their hands. When the boys reached the entrance to Jacob's tent, they came to a halt, puffed up and proud of themselves, and beaming with pleasure at the way they had avenged their family's honor and enriched the family besides.

"You have brought trouble to me by making me odious to the inhabitants of the land," Jacob cried. But the boys were unrepentant. "Should he treat our sister as a harlot?" they asked.

The family was in deep trouble. If the other nations of Canaan united against them—and why shouldn't they, given the provocation of Jacob's sons—the Hebrews would be wiped out. In that dark moment, God came to Jacob. "Arise," he said, "go up to Bethel, and dwell there; and make there an altar to the God who appeared to you when you fled from your brother Esau."

As for Dinah, Genesis does not tell us what became of her. It's probable that she never married: In addition to being the victim of a rape, she was also the sister of ten bloody-minded brothers. What sane man would have wanted the sons of Jacob as his brothers-in-law?

WHAT THE TEN SONS OF JACOB
can teach us

A FRESH OUTRAGE WILL NOT CANCEL OUT AN OLDER ONE

The ten sons of Jacob were not just rude, they were deceitful. In flagrant contempt for the laws of God and man, they incapacitated their enemies the Hivites (who were under the impression that by enduring circumcision they were now the Hebrews' friends), murdered them while they were helpless, plundered their town, stole their livestock, and made slaves of their innocent wives and children. If the sons of Jacob had killed Shechem, they might have been forgiven, but their vengeance was entirely out of proportion, and that is the definition of injustice.

"Why are you downcast, O my soul, and why are you disquieted within me? Hope in God!" (Psalm 42:5)

CONTROL THE KIDS

No matter where you come down on the spanking issue, parents must set limits that their children recognize and obey (at least some of the time). Parents who fail to lay down ground rules of acceptable behavior can look forward to bratty children who grow up to be thoroughly unpleasant, self-mesmerized adults. In the story of Dinah and her brothers it is pretty clear that Jacob was way too indulgent with his sons.

"The rod and reproof give wisdom, but a child left to himself brings shame to his mother." (Proverbs 29:15)

"Fathers, do not provoke your children to anger, but bring them up in the discipline and instruction of the Lord." (Ephesians 6:4)

CHEATING TO GET WHAT YOU WANT IS STILL CHEATING—AND THERE'S NO EXCUSE

"Winning isn't everything—it's the only thing," we've been told. Media, the workplace, just about every component of our culture all drown us in messages of being Number One, above anything else. What those messages imply, of course, is that we can do anything we like in pursuit of coming out on top. Taking advantage of the honesty or innocence or inexperience of the other guy, conning him, scamming him—it's all fair game.

That's how it was in the case of Jacob's sons and the Hivites. The boys knew what outcome they wanted, and they said and did whatever was expedient to get it. Never mind the misery left behind, never mind that they lied and heaped tragedy upon tragedy against so many innocents. They had avenged the honor of their sister, or so they alleged. But since it's unlikely that Dinah ever had any sort of happy life—and we wonder how the brothers could not have foreseen that, given the mores of the time—we are left to wonder what their real motives were. They probably had little to do with love, but a lot to do with winning.

"How long will it be till they are pure in Israel?" (Hosea 8:5)

CHAPTER 6

JOSEPH AND HIS BROTHERS

EVERYBODY HATES A WELL-DRESSED MAN

Genesis 37

Spoiled, conceited, and a snitch besides, Joseph was an unpleasant teenager. But he didn't come into the world that way. His father, Jacob, made it clear to his older sons that Joseph was the favorite child. As proof of his favoritism, he gave Joseph a beautiful coat, the type worn only by nobility. Foolish Jacob. How could he not foresee the misery his thoughtlessness would bring on Joseph and on himself?

No one approves of older brothers piling on their kid brother, ripping off his clothes, throwing him down a dry well, and then selling him to slave traders. But in Joseph's case, his brothers felt that they had their reasons. The 17-year-old Joseph was an insufferable little punk.

It started early. Jacob (as Esau's twin, Jacob has his own history of sibling rivalry) had many children with his wife Leah, and two of his wife's slaves, Bilhah and Zilpah. But his favorite wife, his beloved Rachel, had never given birth. Finally, in Jacob's old age, he learned to his delight that Rachel was pregnant at last. The child was a boy whom the parents named Joseph.

From the day he arrived, Joseph was his father's delight, and he spoiled him. The other boys saw how their father doted on Joseph and that he clearly was their father's favorite. They hated his guts and, as Genesis puts it, "could not speak peaceably to him," which is Bible-speak for tormenting the kid endlessly. And jealous older brothers being what they are, they probably socked Joseph when they were sure no one was looking.

What made it all worthwhile, from Joseph's point of view, was that Daddy still loved him best. And he avenged himself on his brothers in the way little kids have done since the cave man days: He snitched on them at every opportunity. One day, when Joseph was watching the sheep with his brothers, the older boys did something—Genesis doesn't tell us what—that Joseph knew Jacob wouldn't like. Back at the tent that night, Joseph "brought an ill-report of them to his father," which is more Bible-speak for ratting his brothers out.

THE COAT OF MANY COLORS

Immediately after this episode comes the story of the famous coat. If this coat was Jacob's reward to Joseph for informing on his brothers, then Jacob was not simply a doting father, he was a clueless one. How did he expect his other sons to react when they saw their brother dressed like a prince?

And the coat that Jacob gave to Joseph was princely. Current translations of the Bible refer to it as "a long robe with sleeves," but that tame description gives no sense of how fancy the robe was, or the message it sent to Joseph and every other son of Jacob. At that time, only royalty and nobility wore long robes with long sleeves; working men wore practical, short, sleeveless robes that allowed full freedom of movement while they plowed fields or chased off wolves or labored in vineyards. The sleeves alone declared to Jacob's entire clan that Joseph would no longer be expected to break a sweat, that he was a boy of leisure now.

What about the famous "coat of many colors" we learned about when we were kids? As is often the case in English translations of the Old Testament, we loose some of the flavor and meaning of the original Hebrew. The Hebrew text tells us Joseph's robe was made of long strips of fabric, almost certainly of different colors. So those

"Bible Stories for Children" books we all had were actually closer to the Hebrew than many of our contemporary translations of the Scriptures.

Genesis records that Joseph's brothers' reaction was exactly what you would expect: "they hated him."

THE DREAMER

Having turned in his brothers, acquired a magnificent new wardrobe, and essentially retired from the family workforce, Joseph had a pretty high opinion of himself. In an obvious effort to antagonize his brothers, Joseph decided to tell them about one of his dreams. "We were binding sheaves in the field, and lo, my sheaf arose and stood upright; and behold, your sheaves gathered round it, and bowed down to my sheaf." His brothers did not miss the point of his story; in fact, "they hated him yet more for his dreams."

Then Joseph pushed his luck. In the presence of his father and his brothers he recounted yet another dream in which "the sun, the moon, and eleven stars were bowing to me." This time he had gone too far, and even Jacob was irritated with him, "Shall I and your mother and your brothers indeed come to bow ourselves to the ground before you?" That was the last time Joseph regaled the family with his dreams of glory.

There's no denying that Joseph's dreams were egotistical, and certainly that grated on the entire family, including his otherwise indulgent father. Apparently, even in his sleep Joseph couldn't get over himself. But the family's anger was only one piece of the puzzle—they were also unsettled by Joseph's dreams. In ancient Canaan, everyone believed that God (or the gods, in the case of Jacob's pagan neighbors), sent messages to humankind through dreams. The trick was interpreting the dreams correctly so you could understand your destiny, or fulfill whatever it was the Lord wished you to do. Joseph's dreams were understood by his family as a prophecy, that some day he would be lording it over them even more than he did already. That was a distressing thought, even for Jacob.

A SWELL IDEA

Not long after this, Joseph's brothers were out in some distant field with the flocks while he was lounging in the shade of the tent with Jacob. Curious to know if his sons had found good pasturage and water for the sheep and goats, Jacob sent Joseph out to find them, and report back.

Grass and water were scare, so the eldest sons of Jacob had been forced to go a good distance from the family camp, to a place called Dothan, before they found a pasture where the flocks could graze. From far off, the boys could see Joseph coming: Dressed as he was in his splendid coat, there was no mistaking him.

"Here comes this dreamer," one of the boys said.

"Come now," said another, "let us kill him and throw him in one of the pits; then we shall say that a wild beast devoured him and we shall see what becomes of his dreams."

Everyone thought this was a swell idea—everyone except the first-born son, Rueben. "Let us not take his life," Rueben urged his brothers. "Shed no blood; cast him into this pit here in the wilderness, but lay no hand upon him."

Such was the nature of the conversations as Joseph approached his brothers. Not suspecting a thing, he strolled up to them. But before Joseph could say a word, his brothers attacked him, tore off the robe they had come to despise, then hauled him, struggling and screaming for help, to the edge of a dry well. There on the brink, Joseph put up one last fight, but his brothers lifted him off his feet and threw him down the well. Shrieking in terror he fell into the void, then grunted as he struck the bottom.

For a few moments Joseph lay motionless, taking stock: He could tell he was bruised but no bones were broken. Pulling himself to his feet, he looked up. There were his brothers, gathered around the mouth of well, laughing as they sent a shower of dirt and small stones down on him. After they walked away, he could still hear their voices—they were nearby, sitting on the grass, eating their lunch, while Joseph, almost naked and very sore, humiliated and scared, wondered how he would get out of this hole.

TWENTY SHEKELS

Meanwhile, tender-hearted Rueben had wandered off to get a rope so he could come back and rescue Joseph after the rest of the brothers were gone. As Joseph's brothers ate, they heard the far-off tinkling sound of bells. They looked up and, in the distance, saw a caravan of Ishmaelites leading a string of camels laden with balm and myrrh to sell in the markets of Egypt.

The sight of the traders gave Judah an idea. "What profit is it if we slay our brother and conceal his blood?" he said. "Come, let us sell him to the Ishmaelites." Clever Judah—they could get rid of Joseph for good and make a little money besides. Then, as an afterthought, Judah added, "Let not our hand be upon him, for he is our brother, our own flesh."

What a subtle sense of ethics Judah had: Killing their brother would be wrong, but selling him to slave traders just made good business sense. The brothers liked this plan, so they hailed the Ishmaelites, made their offer, and started haggling. In the end, the Ishmaelites paid the sons of Jacob twenty silver shekels for their brother Joseph. Those twenty shekels were worth $12.40 in modern money, divided by ten brothers, every brother got two shekels—$1.24. It doesn't like the sons of Jacob drove a hard bargain, but when you consider that laborers at this time were paid about 16 cents a day, that $1.24 is almost eight days' wages.

So the Ishamelites dropped a rope down to Joseph, drew him up, then tied his hands and led him off to slavery in Egypt.

CROCODILE TEARS

What the brothers needed now was an alibi. They still had the fancy robe they had torn off Joseph's back, all ripped and dirty from the struggle. And once again the sons of Jacob, who had enjoyed a run of good ideas all morning long, had another inspiration. They would kill a goat, dip the torn coat in the goat's blood, and carry it back to their father.

The ten oldest sons of Jacob carried out their deception and a little while later were standing before their father, shedding crocodile tears as they displayed the torn, blood-soaked robe. "This we have found," they said. "See now whether it is your son's robe or not."

"It is my son's robe," Jacob cried. "A wild beast has devoured him; Joseph is without doubt torn to pieces." Heartsick, Jacob went into deep mourning, and neither his wives' nor his daughters' heartfelt attempts to comfort him, nor the feigned efforts of his sons, could console the old man. While Jacob wept and his sons felt smug, Joseph was sold as a slave to an Egyptian military officer, Potiphar, captain of Pharaoh's guard.

Of course, Joseph's story does not end there. He prospered in Potiphar's house, went on to serve the pharaoh, and rose to become the second-most powerful man in Egypt. His separation from his father and his years of slavery were heavy crosses for Joseph to bear, but they matured him. And by permitting Joseph to be carried off to Egypt, God put him in a position where, during a seven-year-long famine, he could save the lives of countless thousands—including his own family.

WHAT JOSEPH
can teach us

GOD HUMBLES THE PROUD

Seventeen-year-old Joseph needed to be taken down a notch—probably several notches. You could argue that selling him into slavery was a bit extreme, but it did the job, knocking the pride right out of him. Joseph became humble, responsible, devout. Severe tribulation reformed his character completely, and so in the eyes of God he was now worthy to be raised higher than he ever would have been had he remained in Canaan. It seems hard to believe when we are in the midst of troubles, sorrows, and the ordinary disappointments of day-to-day life, but they be can be opportunities for self-improvement and for growing closer to God.

"He has put down the mighty from their thrones,
and exalted those of low degree." (Luke 1:52)

BEWARE OF HYPOCRISY
IN YOUR ACTIONS

The grief of the ten sons of Jacob over the "death" of their little brother Joseph appeared to be so genuine that Jacob never caught on. It was an Oscar-winning performance. It was also a lie, one that brought great pain to their father Jacob. Once again, as with the case of the Hivites, the boys had shown contempt for their father and pursued a course of action that made them happy, but caused misery to everyone else. They smiled as Joseph suffered and their father grieved.

Most of us don't commit acts that reach such levels of hypocrisy as Joseph's brothers did. In our lives, hypocritical actions can cause turmoil in ways that are less dramatic, but still very hurtful to those we deceive. When we feel jealousy rising, we need to act quickly—talking with the other person, understanding our feelings, weeding out hatred before it leads us to intentionally mislead innocent, trusting people.

"Behold, God will not reject a blameless man, nor take the hand
of evildoers. He will yet fill your mouth with laughter, and your lips
with shouting. Those who hate you will be clothed with shame."
(Job 8:20–22)

PLAYING FAVORITES WITH YOUR KIDS IS PLAYING WITH FIRE

Showing favoritism to one child over the others is a sure way to tear up a family, although it's not clear from Genesis that Jacob ever learned that lesson. In reading the stories about him, though, we can learn from his mistakes.

Perhaps it's natural for parents to be particularly drawn to children who remind them of themselves, maybe in talent or temperament or goals. But wise parents need to keep those feelings to themselves. Children are quick to pick up slights, and those who realize they aren't the favorites will be deeply hurt and confused. Those feelings can develop into resentment, even hatred, directed against the best-loved child and the parents. Not all situations devolve to the brutality exhibited against Joseph, of course. But if you've ever witnessed interactions among family members who clearly don't get along . . . it's the little day-to-day encounters that suffer under jealousy's rule. The small, loving moments that should be taken for granted are missing, between parents and children, and between siblings. What wise parent would consciously introduce a situation that would bring pain, anger, and hatred into the home?

"If you really fulfill the royal law, according to the scripture, 'You shall love your neighbor as yourself,' you do well. But if you show partiality, you commit sin." (James 2:8–9)

ACCEPT YOUR GOOD FORTUNE GRACEFULLY

Let's be honest—we are all acutely aware of our needs and desires. Some of them, maybe even a lot of them, are normal, necessary, and legitimate. When your needs and desires are more than met, it's hard not to want to shout it from the rooftops. But bragging endlessly about what you have, especially to those who are in need, makes it very difficult for others to be happy for your good fortune.

Joseph had that effect on his family. The Preacher in Ecclesiastes 2:1–11 tends to have that effect on readers of the Bible, too. As those less fortunate continue to struggle and slave, having their noses constantly rubbed in someone else's riches does tend to make them irritable. Eventually, the lucky one will probably find himself ostracized; people can only take so much. Living in the lap of luxury can be a lonely place for those who don't know how to handle it.

"For faith, hope, love abide, these three; but the greatest of these is love." (1 Corinthians 13:13)

TRUST IN GOD'S PLAN FOR THE FUTURE

Joseph's father and older brothers were afraid that if Joseph's dreams came true, they would lose their status in the family and in society. Fear is always with us—fear about our jobs, about money, about our health and the health of members of our family; the list of anxieties seems to get longer with each passing year. But the one thing that conquers fear is faith.

"Therefore do not be anxious saying, 'What shall we eat?' or 'What shall we drink?' or 'What shall we wear?' For the Gentiles seek all these things, and your Father in heaven knows that you need them all. But seek first his kingdom and his righteousness, and all these things shall be yours as well." (Matthew 6:31–33)

CHAPTER 7

SHELOMITH'S SON

WATCH WHAT YOU SAY

Leviticus 24:10–23

The troubles of Shelomith's son were real and far from insignificant, but he let them control his life. He nursed his grudges and his bitterness until finally he turned against God. When he blasphemed, it was as much in hope of injuring God as it was shocking the Israelites. God cannot be injured, but we can do tremendous damage to ourselves, as Shelomith's son too late discovered.

Where there are masters and slaves there are going to be children of mixed race or mixed ethnicity. Sometimes the slave woman was the master's concubine—as in the famous case of Thomas Jefferson and his slave Sally Hemmings (who was herself of mixed race). And sometimes the slave woman was raped by her master. No matter the manner in which they entered the world, in most slave-owning societies the children inherited the condition of their mother. In other words, they were born slaves and remained slaves all their lives; it was a rare thing for a master to emancipate his slave children.

Considering the 430 years the Hebrews were slaves in Egypt, there can be no doubt that a fair number of Hebrew slave children had Egyptian fathers. What a wretched situation for these Hebrew-Egyptian children. First, their father would not recognize them. Second, although they lived as Hebrews slaves among other Hebrew slaves, these ethnically mixed children were not entirely Hebrew: they carried the blood of the hated Egyptian taskmasters. They had some claim to being of the house of Israel, of course, but was it enough of a claim to make them fully welcome? We have no idea. Nor can we say with any certainty, statistically speaking, how many Hebrew-Egyptians Moses led out of Egypt, but the author of Exodus suggests there were a lot of them: "A mixed multitude also went up with them." (Exodus 12.38)

Child psychologists tell us that in some societies or communities, life can be hard for mixed-race children. They may be bullied at school and shunned on the playground. As adults they may find it hard to find work, a place to live, or even a spouse. They don't belong anywhere, and if they don't lapse into depression, there is a good chance that they will lash out in anger at the people who harassed them and isolated them.

THE OUTSIDER

Among "the mixed multitude" Moses led out of Egypt was the son of a Hebrew woman named Shelomith of the tribe of Dan. The boy's father was an Egyptian—most likely Shelomith's master, or perhaps one of her master's sons, or perhaps even one of the Egyptians who worked in her master's household. The author of Exodus does not tell us the name of the Egyptian, but there is an ancient Jewish tradition that says the man was the cruel Egyptian Moses killed. (Exodus 2:11–12) We don't know the name of Shelomith's son, either—no doubt because his crime is so dreadful.

He may have been a happy baby, but as he grew up and began to understand the world into which he had been born, Shelomith's son became an angry, resentful boy. He and his mother were slaves, which was bad enough. What made it worse was seeing his Egyptian father and his Egyptian half-brothers and half-sisters enjoying all the privileges and leisure of free people; they lived in a beautiful house, they had more than enough to eat, and they could spend their days and nights at ease because they had Shelomith, her son, and plenty of other slaves to do all the difficult, unpleasant tasks.

Shelomith raised her son to worship the Lord, but he was almost as angry with God as he was with his Egyptian father. And as for his fellow Hebrews, they tolerated him for his mother's sake. Even among the Danites, his mother's own tribe—and his, too—he felt that he was not entirely welcome.

A HEART FILLED
WITH BITTERNESS

In one respect, at least, Shelomith's son was as Hebrew as the next guy: All the miracles God wrought, all the plagues with which He afflicted the Egyptians, the power He revealed when He liberated the Israelites from slavery and then delivered them one last time from Pharaoh and the Egyptians at the Red Sea—all these things benefited Shelomith's son as much as they did any full-blooded Hebrew. He was free, he would never have to slave for his father again, and he would have his share of milk and honey in the Promised Land.

Sadly, none of this did anything to improve the young man's mood. He was still sullen, still resentful, still difficult and confrontational. He pitched the tent he shared with his mother on the edge of the Danite camp to emphasize that he felt marginalized and unwelcome.

Then one day, Shelomith's son entered the main Israelite camp. On some pretext, he quarreled with a man of full Hebrew descent. The argument escalated until Shelomith's son said the one thing that would be most offensive to the Hebrew—he "blasphemed the Name, and cursed."

To this day, devout Jews never pronounce the Name of God, and it appears likely that this reverent tradition was practiced as early as the Exodus. The shock of hearing the Lord's Name shouted in a dispute, followed by a curse, horrified the Israelites, so much so that they did not know what to do with such an offender. So they seized Shelomith's son and "put him in custody till the will of the Lord should be declared to them."

Why did he do it? Because his heart overflowed with bitterness against his Egyptian father who forced himself on Shelomith, against his Hebrew mother from whom he had inherited the life of a slave, against the Egyptians who treated him as a slave rather than one of their own, and against the Hebrews who at best looked on him as tainted goods. There was no room for the love of God in such a heart. And so when he quarreled with the Israelite, the son of Shelomith did the one thing he knew would shock the Hebrews—he blasphemed. And by his blasphemy, he lashed out against God, too.

The judgment of the Lord against this unhappy young man was severe. "Bring out of the camp him who cursed," God said to Moses, "and let all who heard lay their hands upon his head, and let all the congregation stone him. And say to the people of Israel, Whoever curses his God shall bear his sin."

That same day Moses had the young man taken from the tent that had been his prison. Armed men escorted him outside camp where all the people of Israel had gathered. It was a vast crowd, so big that it would not be possible for everyone to participate in the execution, so only those in the front few rows were armed with stones. The armed men marched the son of Shelomith into the center of the crowd, forced him to his knees, then retreated back into the throng. At a word from Moses, the Israelites raised their arms: A terrible rain of stones fell on Shelomith's son until he was dead.

On the floor of her tent at the edge of the Danite camp, Shelomith sat and wailed.

WHAT SHELOMITH'S SON
can teach us

REVERENCE FOR GOD INCLUDES REVERENCE FOR HIS NAME

It's obvious, but it bears repeating: nothing and no one is holier than God, and His Name is above every other name. Consequently, God deserves our utmost respect and reverence. Perfectly obvious, yet we hear the name of God misused everyday. Remember, then, to teach the kids that to use the Name of God as a curse is a grave sin. Related to it is speaking defiantly or hatefully against God, and using God's name in an oath, vow, or promise made to another which you have no intention of keeping. Love for God is incomplete if it doesn't include love for His Name.

"You shall not take the name of the Lord your God in vain." (Deuteronomy 5:11)

"The fear of the Lord is the beginning of knowledge." (Proverbs 1:7)

WORDS CAN BE WEAPONS

It's never easy to control our passions. Once our blood is up, we start shooting off our mouths—and there's no telling what nastiness will come out. In such situations, reason and restraint go out the window, and in the rapid-fire delivery of hateful, hurtful words, it's not unusual for religion to go, too. What's true about brawling is just as true about a war of words: If someone tries to provoke you, walk away before things get ugly.

"O that a guard were set over my mouth, and a seal of prudence upon my lips, that it may keep me from falling, so that my tongue may not destroy me!" (Sirach 22:27)

DISCRIMINATION IS A SIN, TOO

There is not a person on earth who is not a child of God. Since God is our Father, we are all brothers and sisters in one enormous human family. To hate one of our brothers or sisters because of how they look, how they speak, or where they come from is a crime against the human family and an offense against God. He made us all equal, and gave us all the capacity to know, love, and serve Him in this world.

"Peter rose and said to them, 'Brethren, you know that in the early days God made choice among you, that by my mouth the Gentiles should hear the word of the gospel and believe. And God who knows the heart bore witness to them, giving them the Holy Spirit just as he did to us; and he made no distinction between us and them, but cleansed their hearts by faith.'" (Acts 15:7–9)

"Now there are varieties of gifts, but the same Spirit; and there are varieties of service, but the same Lord; and there are varieties of working, but it is the same God." (1 Corinthians 12:4–6)

OPEN YOUR EYES TO THE GOOD THINGS GOD HAS DONE FOR YOU

From time to time we are all whiners, complaining bitterly about our troubles to our family and friends and coworkers, and even to God. Think of the ten miserable lepers in Luke 17 who begged Jesus to heal them. He did. But of the ten, only one came back to thank the Lord for this tremendous blessing. We can be extremely persistent in prayer when we want something from God, so when He gives it to you, be at least as constant in giving Him thanks. And when you find yourself in the midst of a crisis, give God thanks for the blessings you still enjoy—it's a habit that soothes the soul.

"Thou hast led in thy steadfast love the people whom thou hast redeemed, thou hast guided them by thy strength to thy holy abode." (Exodus 15:13)

CHAPTER 8

THE DAUGHTERS OF MOAB AND MIDIAN

FALSE GODDESSES

Numbers 25

It wasn't right for the teenage boys and young men of Israel to take up with the teenage girls and young women of Moab and Midian. But as bad as that was, the sin that really offended the Lord was the worship of the Canaanite gods, particularly the vile Baal-Peor. It's a lesson the young men learned the hard way—and too late.

For parents, the statistics are very disturbing. According to the American Academy of Pediatrics, approximately one in three fourteen-year-olds have had sex. By the time the kids are seventeen or eighteen, approximately seven out of ten have had sex. And in many cases, this sexual activity is not a one-shot deal—it is a pattern of promiscuous behavior.

Teenagers have lots of reasons for taking on many sexual partners: it makes them feel like adults; it enables them to fit in with friends who are sexually active; it is an assertion that they have grown up and now they are free to do whatever they like. But teenagers won't talk about their emotional immaturity, or their increased risk of becoming infected with a sexually transmitted disease, or discovering that a baby is on its way. For parents who grew up in a society where sex among grammar school kids was unheard of and sex among high school kids was rare, this sudden outbreak of sexual activity among children and teens is shocking, not to mention worrying.

Among the ancient Moabites and the Midianites, however, sex at any age was not a big deal. They worshipped gods and goddesses of fertility—and not just the fertility of the crops. Some temples offered worshippers an almost endless selection of sacred prostitutes, male and female. It was an activity that was sort of like a fund-raiser: The money worshippers paid to the sacred prostitutes was passed along to the priests who used it to keep the temple in good repair. Sex, in the pagan societies of the Middle East, was just a form of recreation.

The people of Israel, however, did not take sex lightly. Obedient to the commandments, they believed sex was only permitted within marriage. Of course, some Israelites strayed, having premarital and extramarital flings, but only the most callous pretended that what he or she was doing wasn't an offense against God and a violation of the laws of Israel.

ALL IN THE FAMILY

The Israelites' forty years of wandering in the desert were nearly over; the Promised Land lay just across the Jordan, and all of the Lord's promises were about to be fulfilled. But the people hadn't crossed over the Jordan yet, and the lands where they were staying, Moab and Midian, were no place for God-fearing people.

The Moabites traced their nation back to Moab, the son produced during Lot's drunken night of lust with his eldest daughter. Since Lot was Abraham's nephew, the Moabites were related to the Israelites. Unlike the people of Israel, however, the people of Moab did not worship God. They adored the whole pantheon of Canaanite gods, including gods who demanded human sacrifice—even the sacrifice of small children. The Moabites even had a god, Baal-Peor, that was associated with excrement. Given the unsavory beginnings of these people in that cave above the smoking ruins of Sodom and Gomorrah, what could you expect of the Moabites?

Also in the neighborhood were the Midianites, who were related to the people of Israel as well. They were descended from Abraham's son Midian by his concubine Keturah. After Moses killed the Egyptian he fled into the desert and found sanctuary in the camp of the Midianite priest Jethro, and in time Moses married Jethro's daughter, Zipporah. In general, the Midianites worshipped the same gods as the Moabites, but it's possible that Jethro and his family worshipped the God of Israel.

Officially, the Moabites were hostile to the Israelites. When Moses led his people across the border into Moab, the king sent out a prophet named Balaam to curse the Israelites. The Moabites' reputation as morally corrupt enemies of God caused Boaz to think twice before marrying the Moabite widow Ruth. And whenever the prophets wished to make a point about people whose pride, vices, and heathenish wickedness were off the charts, they referred to Moab and Moabites.

All their lives the teenage boys and unmarried young men in the camp had known nothing but wandering in the desert. Now they were in a pleasant country near the Jordan River. But as nice as the river valley was, far nicer were the teenage girls and young women of Moab and Midian, who were as eager to meet the Israelite guys as the guys were to meet them.

IN THE MOOD FOR LOVE

The Israelites encamped at a place in Moab called Shittim, which means "the grove of acacia trees." All their lives the teenage boys and unmarried young men in the camp had known nothing but wandering in the desert. Now they were in a pleasant country near the Jordan River. But as nice as the river valley was, far nicer were the teenage girls and young women of Moab and Midian, who were as eager to meet the Israelite guys as the guys were to meet them.

The young Israelites made a point of going far from the camp, where their watchful parents and the watchful priests could not see them making new friends with the lovely young Moabites and Midianites. The young Israelites were in the mood for romantic adventure and freedom from parental supervision; one thing led to another and soon the boys "began to play the harlot with the daughters of Moab."

That stirred up the wrath of the Lord. It is one thing to be seduced by a pretty face, but to be seduced into turning away from the God of Israel for something as vile as Baal-Peor—for that, there can be no excuse.

Having won over the boys and young men of Israel by using the oldest trick in the book, the Moabites and Midianites invited their new boyfriends to a festival. There would be food and wine, music and dancing, and oh yeah—there would be bowing down before false gods.

The Israelite guys went happily to the festival, where they ate their fill and then some (they were at the age when their metabolism

THE DAUGHTERS OF MOAB AND MIDIAN: FALSE GODDESSES

was in overdrive). Then they joined the daughters of Moab and Midian in adoring the gods of Canaan, especially the disgusting god, Baal-Peor.

That stirred up the wrath of the Lord. It is one thing to be seduced by a pretty face, but to be seduced into turning away from the God of Israel for something as vile as Baal-Peor—for that, there can be no excuse. God spoke to Moses, commanding that the young men who worshipped Baal-Peor must be hanged. So Moses informed the judges of Israel: "Every one of you slay his men who have yoked themselves to Baal of Peor."

The use of the word "yoked" is interesting. It suggests a marriage or at least a union such as the young men of Israel and the young women of Moab and Midian engaged in, but it also implies a form of slavery, and the Israelites had engaged in that, too, when they fell down before the grotesque idol of Baal-Peor.

And so, to the grief of the young Israelites families and their Moabite and Midianite girlfriends, the judges of the tribes rounded up the foolish young men and hanged them.

ZIMRI AND COXBI

After the executions, the Israelite camp was a tense place. No one ventured out for fear of being enticed by a Moabite or a Midianite to repeat the foolhardy behavior of the young men who had just been hanged. But one Israelite man was not dismayed. Zimri came and went as he always had, and associated with any of the Moabites or Midianites he encountered.

One day Zimri returned to the camp with a beautiful Midianite woman named Coxbi. He paraded her "in the sight of Moses and in the sight of the whole congregation of the people of Israel." The people were stunned by Zimri's audacity. And when he took her to meet his parents, the people felt nothing but pity for the family.

After making the introduction, the couple retired to Zimri's tent where they could have some privacy. All this was too much for Phinehas, the grandson of Aaron. Seizing a javelin, he ran into Zimri's tent where he skewered both of the lovers with a single spear-thrust.

THE DAUGHTERS OF MOAB AND MIDIAN: FALSE GODDESSES

WHAT THE DAUGHTERS
OF MOAB AND MIDIAN
can teach us

CONSIDER WHERE THE OTHER
PERSON IS COMING FROM

There is a tendency to regard the young women of Moab and Midian as harlots, but that's not fair. By the standards of their society, these young women weren't doing anything wrong. Recreational sex was only recreational sex. Besides, it might be the first step toward marriage, which would be nice. If it didn't lead to marriage, that was alright, too. In the case of the young men of Israel, though, they had a different set of standards—and they were unfaithful to them.

"He who is of God hears the words of God." (John 8:47)

KEEP NAUGHTY PEOPLE
AT ARM'S LENGTH

Have you noticed that bad behavior is always so much cooler than good behavior? It's tough enough for mature adults to resist the allure of taking a walk on the wild side, but for those in their teens and twenties, it can seem impossible. The best solution is to keep away from people whose standards and values are sharply at variance with your own. You don't have to call down fire and brimstone upon them. Just be pleasant and decline their invitations.

"For surely it is not with angels that he is concerned but with the descendants of Abraham. Therefore he had to be made like his brethren in every respect, so that he might become a merciful and faithful high priest in the service of God, to make expiation for the sins of the people." (Hebrews 2:16–17)

AS THE PARENT, YOU DO KNOW BETTER

There is no substitute for a good upbringing. Give a kid the essential information about right and wrong and what the Lord expects, and he or she will at least be able to gauge what is at risk when a wayward friend or acquaintance makes an improper suggestion. Kids being what they are—curious, eager to experiment, a little defiant from time to time—there is no guarantee that they will always do what is right. But at least you haven't sent them out into the world totally defenseless.

"You shall worship the Lord your God and him only shall you serve." (Matthew 4:10)

CHAPTER 9

MICAH THE EPHRAIMITE

HEATHEN CHEMISTRY

Judges 17–18

There is a kind of rough justice in the story of Micah the Ephraimite: He stole from his mother, the army of Danites stole from him. In addition to the "what goes around comes around" moral of this story, we also get a vivid picture of religious chaos in the land of Israel. People could pick and choose among beliefs as they liked; following the Commandments was optional. And Micah, the agile liar and thief, had the chance to learn how it felt when the tables were turned.

Y ou walk into the kitchen where you find your child pouring the contents of your change purse into his pocket. He's scared now because he's been caught red-handed. You're mad because you give the little darling almost everything his heart desires, yet here he is, rifling through your purse, stealing your money.

It's an upsetting scenario, but here's a little reassurance: Children who pilfer loose change from their parents are not charter members of the Future Felons of America club. Kids steal for lots of reasons—a desire to have more control over their life, to keep up with their friends who are stealing and extol the thrill of it, to get your attention, or for the simple reason that the money was laying out there and they couldn't resist the temptation. Whatever the kid's reason, pocketing a few coins that don't belong to him does not mean he is doomed to a life of crime.

LIGHT-FINGERED,
BUT QUICK-WITTED

Micah the Ephraimite did more than filch a few pennies from his mother; he walked away with a cool eleven hundred pieces of silver. And he got away with it. No one suspected him of the theft. But when his mother began calling down curses on the thief, Micah got nervous—he didn't want those curses to alight on him (apparently Micah's mother had a real gift for vividly descriptive imprecations). Rather than risk a sudden eruption of an unsightly skin rash, or having body parts suddenly drop off one by one, Micah thought it best to return the money to Mom. But how best to return it? That was Micah's problem. If he admitted that he had been the thief, she'd still be angry, and her curses would probably remain in force. So Micah decided to cast himself as a hero who tracked down the thief and recovered his mother's missing fortune, no doubt at great risk to his own life.

His mother was still raging over the theft when Micah put his plan into action. "The eleven hundred pieces of silver which were taken from you," he said, "about which you uttered a curse, and also spoke it in my ears, behold, the silver is with me; I took it." What Micah meant was that he took the silver back from the mysterious thief.

Micah's mother was, understandably, delighted. "Blessed be my son by the Lord!" she exclaimed. And as her light-fingered, quick-witted son poured the eleven hundred silver pieces into her hands, the grateful woman declared, "I consecrate the silver to the Lord from my hand for my son."

So far the story is of a cunning thief who has thoroughly bamboozled his victim. But then the story of Micah and his mother takes an unexpected turn.

"EVERY MAN DID WHAT WAS RIGHT
IN HIS OWN EYES"

Micah's mother's notion of how to honor the Lord was peculiar. Taking two hundred of her silver pieces, she visited a silversmith and instructed him to melt down the silver and fashion an idol of a false god. The finished piece Micah set up in the family home, turning one room into a shrine. To dress up their private chapel, Micah made his own ephod, a knee-length sleeveless vestment worn by a high priest; he also made teraphim, small idols of various gods that the pagans of Canaan worshipped on little altars in their homes.

From gratitude to the Lord for restoring her stolen money to her, Micah's mother had segued to turning her house into a pagan temple. But the shrine was incomplete, it needed one thing more: a Levite, a priest to tend the shrine, receive offerings from the worshippers, and make sacrifices.

By chance at this precise time, a Levite from Bethlehem left his home and went wandering. Eventually he found his way to Micah's house, and when the young man learned that the stranger was a Levite, he was delighted. "Stay with me, and be to me a father and a priest," Micah said, "and I will give you ten pieces of silver a year, and a suit of apparel, and a living." This was an offer the Levite could not refuse. He signed on as Micah's chaplain. "Now I know that the Lord will prosper me," Micah said, "because I have a Levite as priest."

What a hodge-podge! Micah and his mother believed in the God of Israel, but they also believed in the false gods of the Canaanites. The Levite was dedicated to the service of the Lord, yet he was willing to take a job as a pagan priest. But this inconsistency pops up time and again in the Old Testament: Rachel stole and hid the teraphim, or household gods, that belonged to her father, Laban; Michal put a human-sized teraphim in David's bed to lead her father, Saul, into believing the young man had not escaped; as part of his religious reform, King Josiah destroyed every teraphim he could lay his hands on.

Apparently many ancient Israelites remained committed, in their own fashion, to the God of their fathers. Worshipping him, maintaining the covenant with him, were essential aspects of the Israelites' identity. At the same time, many of them couldn't resist the attraction of the gods of their Canaanite neighbors.

The only explanation is that the times of the judges were wild and wooly days in Israel, when both the religious and the political life of the people was chaotic. Or as the author of Judges put it, "In those days there was no king in Israel; every man did what was right in his own eyes."

"UNDER THE EYE OF THE LORD"

When the 12 tribes of Israel divvyed up the Promised Land, the tribe of Dan had been shorted; they had no portion of land assigned to them. Of necessity, they became nomads as their ancestors had been, but they were getting tired of their rootless existence—they wanted a home. So the leaders of the Danites selected five able men to explore the country and find a likely place where the people of Dan could settle, or conquer if necessary.

Micah and his mother must have lived along a major highway because, just like the wandering Levite, the five Danite real estate developers found their way to the family's door, too. As they rested in the house, the Danites heard a familiar voice coming from the room that had become the household shrine. Micah's Levite was an old friend of the Danites, and while they were surprised to find him in the country of Ephraim, from a practical point of view they were also pleased to see him. "Inquire of God, we pray thee," the Danites said, "that we may know whether the journey on which we are setting out will succeed." The Levite did as his friends asked, and whether it was through genuine prayer to the Lord or through unlawful divination, he reported back, "Go in peace. The journey on which you go is under the eye of the Lord."

THE CREAM PUFFS OF LAISH

Micah's houseguests did not consider making a portion of the land of Ephraim their home; this mountainous region west of the Jordan River did not appeal to them. The next morning the five Danites continued their search for a suitable homeland for their tribe, and when they reached the shores of the Mediterranean Sea, they found the perfect site. Located beside the sea, the town of Laish was populated by "quiet and unsuspecting" people who possessed great wealth, as well as a fertile, well-watered territory, so that they were "lacking nothing that is in the earth." In all their travels the Danites had never seen any spot so lovely and so productive, or native inhabitants who would be so easy to conquer.

Mission accomplished, the five scouts returned to their fellow Danites. "Arise!" they said, "and let us go up against them."

So with 600 men armed to the teeth, the Danites headed off to wage war against a town full of cream puffs. Predictably, their way led them past Micah's house. As they approached, the five scouts told their fellow soldiers that in Micah's house was a shrine with idols and a Levite to minister in the tiny temple. It seemed to the Danites that in their new home they would need gods and a Levite. While the armed 600 waited at the gate, the five scouts brazenly entered Micah's house and made straight for the shrine, which they began to dismantle.

"What are you doing?" the house Levite asked.

"Keep quiet," the five Danites answered, "put your hand upon your mouth, and come with us, and be to us a father and a priest.

Is it better for you to be priest to the house of one man, or be priest to a tribe and family in Israel?"

This was an even better offer than the one Micah had made to the Levite. He agreed to come with the Danites, and even packed up the idols and the ephod himself.

The Levite and his new Danite congregation were some distance from the house when Micah came chasing after them. Once he caught up, Micah confronted the Danites. "You take my gods which I made, and the priest, and go away, and what have I left?"

It was gutsy of one young guy to accuse a small but heavily armed army of theft, but it wasn't especially wise. The five scouts encouraged Micah to be a bit more discrete. "Do not let your voice be heard among us," they cautioned, "lest angry fellows fall upon you, and you lose your life with the life of your household."

Outnumbered and outgunned, Micah had no option but to let go of his private Levite, and his mother's silver idol, and the lesser idols, and all the fancy furnishings of his house temple. Galling though it was, this was a prudent decision, because the Danites were spoiling for a fight. At Laish they fell upon those poor, "quiet and unsuspecting" people and killed them all.

After the battle, the Levite who had worked for Micah set up an altar for the silver idol Micah's mother had ordered from the local silversmith, and it became the Danites' god.

WHAT MICAH THE EPHRAIMITE
can teach us

GOD IS FAITHFUL EVEN WHEN WE ARE NOT

In Revelation 3:20, the Lord says, "Behold, I stand at the door and knock." The door is the human heart, and Lord's knocking is His call for us to repent, to open up our hearts and let His grace flow in. Everyone falls short of living the life of the gospels, of fulfilling the commandments of God, but He does not strike us down when we fail. God's mercy pursues us, calling us back to our true home.

"Trust in the Lord forever, for the Lord God is an everlasting rock."
(Isaiah 26:4)
"O give thanks to the Lord of lords, for his steadfast love
endures forever." (Psalm 136:3)

THERE ARE ABSOLUTES

To Micah and his mother, to the Levite and the Danites, one god was as good another. Today we call that relativism. It is a school of thought that argues there is no absolute truth, no standard of right and wrong, no way of knowing how to please God—all of which is just another way of saying that there are no consequences if we spend our lives seeking only to please ourselves. We may be looking through a glass darkly now, but there are a few things we can know with certainty, and we cling to them.

"Let not loyalty and faithfulness forsake you; bind them around your
neck, write them on the tablet of your heart. So that you will find
favor and good repute in the sight of God and man." (Proverbs 3:3)

DON'T CONFUSE LICENTIOUSNESS
WITH LIBERTY

God created us free to chose between good and evil. We want to do good, but there are so many occasions when we drop the ball and make bad choices. If we persist in choosing bad over good, eventually we are no longer free. We have become slaves to sin, as Paul puts it in Romans 6:17.

The story of Micah mentions a silver idol that became his family's household god; today, the most popular idol may be the pursuit of our own pleasure, without regard to the cost to ourselves or anyone else. For our own sakes, it's wise to remember that even freedom must have limits; otherwise, it is anarchy.

"For whoever does the will of my Father in heaven is my brother, and sister, and mother." (Matthew 12:50)

"Now therefore, if you will obey my voice and keep my covenant, you shall be my own possession among all peoples." (Exodus 19:5)

ABIMELECH

THE SINS OF THE SON

Judges 8:31–9:57

When Israel was governed by judges, God alone was their king. But Abimelech, the son of Gideon, wanted power over his fellow Israelites and would permit nothing, not even family ties, to get in his way. The story of Abimelech reveals what happens when a man tries to usurp the authority that belongs to God.

CHAPTER 10

Gideon was lucky. He died before his boy Abimelech started acting up.

The story of Abimelech is another example of a child who rejects the good example of his father, who rebels against God, and tries to make himself the ultimate authority.

It started around the time he was three years old. Abimelech was the bossy kid in the village, the one who, in an aggressive tone of voice, ordered the other kids around, and even tried to give orders to his mother and father. It's cute initially, but having a three-year-old dictator in the house gets old fast.

Maybe Gideon and Abimelech's mother (Judges does not tell us her name) followed the standard, recommended methods for correcting bossiness in a small child: telling him that if he wants something, he must ask politely; taking him aside during a play date to remind him that if he doesn't share the toys with the other kids, he is going home; complimenting him when he was polite to adults and let other kids pick the games. If these were the techniques Abimelech's parents tried, it's clear that they didn't work.

Of course, it's not a sure thing that a child who is strong-willed will grow up to be a fascist. A bossy three-year-old may mature into a self-starter, an entrepreneur, a visionary. That happy outcome requires parental direction early on, too, and once again in Abimelech's case, it didn't pan out. Instead of growing up to be the Old Testament's equivalent to Bill Gates, he became a pint-sized Benito Mussolini.

SCRAMBLING TO THE TOP

Gideon had many wives, with whom he had 70 sons. He also had a concubine, and she was the mother of Abimelech. In the family hierarchy of the time, Gideon's sons by his wives outranked any son he had with a concubine. If he wished, he could will property and money to his children by his concubine, and perhaps he did leave something to Abimelech. If there was such a bequest, it wasn't enough for Abimelech: He had his eye on the whole enchilada.

Abimelech's mother was from Shechem, the town that, centuries earlier, Jacob's ten sons had attacked to avenge the rape of their sister, Dinah. It was a wealthy place, full of hardworking merchants who traded in olive oil, wheat, grapes, and livestock. After the death of Gideon, Abimelech traveled to Shechem where he gathered together all of his mother's family and relatives and let them in on his plan: He wanted to be king over the people of Israel.

At that time, Israel was governed by judges; the people regarded God as their king. Gideon had been a judge, and it was probable, now that he was dead, that one of his 70 sons would become judge in his place. Such a smooth, peaceful transition did not suit Abimelech's purposes, so, to spread uneasiness among the people of Shechem, he sent out his relatives through the town to spread a rumor that Israel was about to fall under the lawless sway of all 70 of the sons of

ABIMELECH: THE SINS OF THE SON

Gideon. To everyone who heard the rumor, that sounded like a recipe for governmental pandemonium, but Abimelech offered a sane alternative—the people of Shechem could make him king. And once they did make him king, they could expect preferential treatment because, as Abimelech reminded the people of Shechem, "I am your bone and your flesh."

This plan appealed especially to Abimelech's relatives, who liked the idea of becoming a royal family. They all chipped in and gave Abimelech 70 pieces of silver so he could hire an escort suitable for a man who would be king. With the money, Abimelech "hired worthless and reckless fellows," thoroughly unsuitable as an entourage for royalty, but just the sort of men Abimelech would need for the next stage of his scramble to the top.

THE PARABLE OF THE TREES

With his Shechem home boys, Abimelech returned to Gideon's house in Ophrah where all 70 of his half-brothers lived together. At night, while the household was asleep, Abimelech's gang broke into the house, and dragged the sons of Gideon outside. In the courtyard of the house stood a large stone; on that stone, by the flashing light of many torches, Abimelech slaughtered his half-brothers, one by one, until the stone was slick with blood and the ground was saturated with it. Only one son of Gideon escaped—Jotham, the youngest, who found a hiding place and remained concealed there until the massacre was over and Abimelech and his band of criminals had left. Then the boy crept from his hiding place and fled into the countryside.

Back at Shechem, Abimelech's relatives and the other citizens of the town had prepared a coronation ceremony. With as much pomp as the town could afford, they led him in a procession to an oak tree outside the city walls where there was a pillar erected in honor of the Canaanite god, Baal-berith, also known as Beel-zebub, the notorious lord of the flies. In this unholy place, the people of Shechem placed a golden crown on Abimelech's head and proclaimed him king.

They were still cheering their new lord when the clear, high voice of a boy rose above the clamor. Looking about, they saw Jotham standing a little above them on Mount Gerizim. "Listen to me, you men of Shechem," the boy cried, "that God may listen to you." When the crowd had grown still, Jotham told them a parable of how all the trees had decided to find one special tree to anoint as their king. The trees approached the olive tree, the fig tree, and even the grape vine, but none of these good, useful plants would accept the trees' invitation to "Come you, and reign over us."

Finally the trees approached the bramble with the same offer they had made to the olive, the fig, and the vine. "If in good faith you are anointing me king over you," the bramble replied, "then come and take refuge in my shade."

The bramble, of course, represented Abimelech, from whom the people of Shechem could expect as much comfort as a bramble could provide shade on a hot day—in other words, none at all. Nor did the people of Shechem deserve good things. Jotham reminded them, "My father fought for you, and risked his life, and rescued you from the hand of Midian; and you have risen up against my father's house this day, and have slain his sons, seventy men on one stone, and have made Abimelech, the son of his maidservant, king over the citizens of Shechem because he is your kinsman."

The crowd was getting restless, and Abimelech's gang was itching for him to give the sign so they could run up the hill and slit Jotham's throat. The boy knew he was running out of time, so he delivered one final parting shot. "Let fire come out of Abimelech, and devour the citizens of Shechem and Bethmillo; and let fire come out of the citizens of Shechem and from Bethmillo, and devour Abimelech."

A roar of anger rumbled up from the crowd, and Abimelech gave his bodyguards the order to kill Jotham. But the boy was already off

ABIMELECH: THE SINS OF THE SON

and running to his next hiding place where, once again, Abimelech's people could not find him.

THE HONEYMOON IS OVER

Aside from the fact that he was kin, exactly what the people of Shechem found appealing about Abimelech remains a mystery. But whatever his appeal was, it didn't last long: Abimelech was grasping, violent, vengeful, unpredictable, and unjust. He had been king for only three years when the people of Shechem decided they had had their fill of their royal cousin. They schemed to ambush Abimelech, and when they weren't scheming, they manned the mountain passes where they robbed travelers. In other words, lawlessness had descended upon the land, and Abimelech, it appeared, was powerless to do anything about it. This made the people of Shechem cocky.

Autumn came and the farmers harvested their grapes, crushed them, and made wine. To celebrate a bountiful crop, they rolled their barrels of new wine to the temple of Baal-berith, set up tables inside the sanctuary and cooking fires out in the courtyard, and held a harvest festival.

As the wine flowed and the people drank more deeply, they became bolder. Or dumber. Definitely they became less discrete. One man named Gaal, a newcomer to the town who had only recently arrived in Shechem with all his relatives, made the most noise. Rising from his couch (although he was a bit unsteady on his feet), Gaal asked his neighbors, "Who is Abimelech, and who are we of Shechem, that we should serve him?"

It was a good question. Too bad no one had thought to ask it three years earlier when they all clamored for Abimelech to be their king.

Aside from the fact that he was kin, exactly what the people of Shechem found appealing about Abimelech remains a mystery. But whatever his appeal was, it didn't last long.

Gaal knocked back another cup of wine, then added, his speech a bit more slurred than the last time he spoke, "Would that this people were under my hand! Then I would remove Abimelech. I would say to Abimelech, 'Increase your army, and come out.'"

Great. The people of Shechem could replace the bloody Abimelech with a wine-soaked braggart.

"WHERE IS YOUR MOUTH NOW?"

Among those present at the harvest festival was Zebul, the mayor of Shechem, and a man loyal to Abimelech (heaven knows why). Zebul had also been hitting the wine hard, but not as hard as Gaal who, in his booze-addled condition, had preached treason to his neighbors, suggested they bump off Abimelech, and offered himself as their next king. Zebul sent a message to Abimelech that there was talk of deposing him, and that Gaal was the ringleader. "Now therefore, go by night," Zebul advised the king, "you and the men that are with you, and lie in wait in the fields. Then in the morning, as soon as the sun is up, rise early and rush upon the city; and when he and the men that are with him come out against you, you may do to them as occasion offers." It was night when Abimelech received Zebul's message, but he roused his army and marched on Shechem, taking up positions on the mountain above the town.

The next morning Gaal, his stomach churning and his head pounding, rolled off his couch in the temple and staggered out to the city gate for some air. Zebul, who was not hung over, followed him.

As Gaal stood at the open gate, breathing deeply of the clean morning air, hoping it would clear his head, he saw something move on the mountain. "Look," he said to Zebul, "men are coming down from the mountaintops!"

Zebul scoffed. "You see the shadow of the mountains as if they were men," he answered.

Gaal felt thoroughly rotten that morning; perhaps, along with all of his other symptoms, his eyes were playing tricks on him, too. But then he saw, very clearly, an army on the plain outside the town. This could be no hallucination. "Look," he said to Zebul, "men are coming down from the center of the land, and one company is coming from the direction of the Diviner's Oak."

Now Zebul stopped playing with Gaal's head. "Where is your mouth now," he asked, "you who said, 'Who is Abimelech that we should serve him?' Are not these the men whom you despised? Go out now and fight with them."

Running back into the city, Gaal called for the men of Shechem to arm themselves and meet at the city gate. When the men stood armed and ready to fight, Gaal led them out against Abimelech's army. The men of Shechem were merchants, and potters, and farmers; the king had professional soldiers. In very little time Abimelech's army defeated and scattered the men of Shechem, who threw down their weapons and ran with all their might for the safety of their city's walls. Gaal was among the survivors who made it back to Shechem, where Zebul was waiting for him. With his own guard, he arrested Gaal and all of his relatives, then drove them out of the city, and bolted the gates behind them. On the plains surrounding Shechem, as the neighbors looked on from the ramparts, Gaal and his family were all killed by Abimelech's troops.

THE LAST STAND

The next morning the guards in the watchtowers announced that Abimelech and his men were gone. The guards were wrong; the king and his army were hiding. When the farmers, thinking it was safe, opened the gates and went out to work in the fields, the king's army rushed from their hiding places, massacred the farmers, then surged through the open gates of Shechem and began to kill the entire population.

One thousand men, women, and children fled to the citadel, the Tower of Shechem, the city's stronghold. Rather than pursue them, the king took an axe and walked to Mount Zalmon where he cut and bundled up brushwood. Turning to his bewildered soldiers he said, "What you have seen me do, make haste to do, as I have done." So every man in the army cut a bundle of brushwood, then followed the king back to the city. There, Abimelech commanded them to pile the brushwood against the base of the Tower of Shechem, then light it. The dry brushwood caught, and soon huge flames engulfed the tower. No one inside escaped the conflagration.

A WOMAN WITH A MILLSTONE

Shechem was not the only town to rebel against Abimelech: Thebez, nearby, also revolted against the king, so he marched on that town next.

When the people of Thebez saw Abimelech's army approaching their city, they fled into their citadel tower where many men and women climbed out onto the roof to rain down arrows and javelins

ABIMELECH: THE SINS OF THE SON

on their attackers. Abimelech was not concerned—he would clear Thebez of rebels the same way he had cleared Shechem. He was riding up to the base of the tower to give the order to burn it, when a woman on the tower roof lifted a millstone above her head and hurdled it down at the king. The stone struck Abimelech's skull, knocking him off his horse. As he lay dying in the street, Abimelech called his armor-bearer. "Draw your sword and kill me," he said, "lest men say of me, 'A woman killed him.'" The armor-bearer did as the king commanded.

When the army saw that Abimelech was dead, they stopped the attack on Thebez and each man went back to his home.

The author of Judges concludes, "Thus God requited the crime of Abimelech, which he committed against his father in killing his seventy brothers; and God also made all the wickedness of the men of Shechem fall back upon their heads."

WHAT ABIMELECH
can teach us

THE WISEST LEADERS KNOW THAT GOD RULES OVER ALL

In the family, at school, on the job, in government, there is a hierarchy of who is in charge. But we must always remember that God is at the top of the heap, as the ultimate ruler and judge. Everyone who has authority eventually reports to Him. And anyone in a leadership position—parents, teachers, managers, supervisors, and government officials of all varieties—should take a deep breath and remember their place in the hierarchy when they make any decision, great or small. Those decisions will be responsible and good when made in the spirit of God's law.

"Teach me good judgment and knowledge,
for I believe in thy commandments." (Psalm 119:66)

"If you cry out for insight and raise your voice for understanding,
if you seek it like silver and search for it as for hidden treasures;
then you will understand the fear of the Lord and find the knowledge
of God. For the Lord gives wisdom; from his mouth come
knowledge and understanding." (Proverbs 2:3-6)

LEADERS WHO DEAL TREACHEROUSLY WITH OTHERS WILL BEHAVE THAT WAY TO THEIR OWN PEOPLE

Abimelech began his bid for royal power by massacring 69 of his 70 brothers. This should have been a clue for the people of Shechem that their would-be king would bring them nothing but trouble and pain. Why did they still go along? Why did they crown such a blood-thirsty scoundrel king?

The answer is self-interest. Time and again, Bible history and secular history show us vivid examples of nations that turned a blind eye to the clear signs that the man (or woman) who wanted to rule them was a depraved maniac. Yet for the sake of self-interest, for a shot at getting a little more than the next guy, they put themselves under the authority of a tyrant. Of course, when that leader turns out to be a Nero, or an Ivan the Terrible, or a Hitler, or a Mao, then everyone wails and wonders how they got into such a mess. The signs were there at the beginning.

"The name of the Lord is a strong tower; the righteous man runs into it and is safe." (Proverbs 18:10)

"For You have been a shelter for me, a strong tower from the enemy." (Psalm 61:3)

"Every good tree produces good fruit, but a rotten tree produces bad fruit." (Matthew 7:17)

THE WICKED PROSPER FOR
A BRIEF TIME ONLY

The good news is that Nero, and Ivan the Terrible, and Hitler, and Mao are all gone. The Soviet empire, which looked like it would last forever (certainly the guys in the Kremlin hoped so), crumbled in about 70 years. Twelve years after Hitler came to power in Germany, the Third Reich lay in ruins. Evil empires are ultimately self-destructive. Driven by everything that is bad, the implacable enemy of everything and everyone who is good, these corrupt regimes have a way of uniting people of good will to resist them. The victory may not come fast, or as painlessly as we would like, but in the end, it always comes.

"He will swallow up death forever, and the Lord God will wipe away tears from all faces, the reproach of his people he will take away from all the earth, for the Lord has spoken." (Isaiah 25:8)

"Lord, to whom shall we go? You have the words of eternal life."
(John 6:68)

CHAPTER 11

HOPHNI AND PHINEHAS

AN UNHOLY ALLIANCE

1 Samuel 2:12–17, 22–25, 27–34, 4:1–18

The story of Hophni and Phinehas, the godless, hypocritical sons of the high priest Eli, teaches us many lessons: about parents who from a misguided idea of what constitutes affection fail to correct their children, about clergy who disgrace their office and bring shame upon believers, about basically good people who turn a blind eye when they see someone exploit the church.

W e've seen this scenario before: The parents are devout, upright, and deeply involved in their church; their kids reject God, the gospel, and will not set foot inside a sanctuary. It is a situation that causes a great deal of tension in a religious family, and puts the parents through the wringer of self-examination. What did they do wrong? When did they set a bad example? But the fact is, it is rarely Mom and Dad's fault. For some people, the "freedom" of the world has always been more attractive than the practice of the faith.

But we can say one thing for kids who reject their family's church outright—at least they show some integrity. Much worse is the shameless hypocrite who enters the ministry to fleece the Lord's sheep. Sadly, that was the experience of Eli, a holy old man, a direct descendant of Aaron, the brother of Moses. Eli had spent his entire life as a sincere, faithful priest of the Lord. Furthermore, for 40 years he served as a judge in Israel, and high priest of the sanctuary at Shiloh. Eli is best known as the foster father of the boy Samuel, who grew up to be one of Israel's greatest prophets.

What had this good old man ever done to deserve two sons like Hophni and Phinehas?

You can imagine the kind of children they were: rarely playing, but forever scheming; picking on the little kids and fighting with the older kids in the neighborhood; defying their teachers; showing no respect to their elders; and hanging out with the worst troublemakers in town. Whenever Hophni and Phinehas swaggered by, the town gossips put their heads together, clucked their tongues, and lamented that "No good will come of those two." And for once, the gossips were right on the money.

WORTHLESS MEN

The priesthood was hereditary in ancient Israel—you could say it was a family business. But while Eli fulfilled his sacred office with care and true dedication, Hophni and Phinehas had figured out how to play all the angles. Or as the sacred author put it, "Now the sons of Eli were worthless men; they had no regard for the Lord."

Every time an Israelite came to Shiloh to offer a sacrifice to God, Hophni and Phinehas would send their servants to demand a portion of the slaughtered lamb or goat or bull for their private pantry. Naturally, many Israelites were shocked and offended by the boldness of these priests, but if they resisted, the servants of Hophni and Phinehas took their meat by force. Since nobody wanted to leave the sanctuary with a bloody nose or a black eye, the faithful got in the habit of swallowing their pride and handing over whatever the sons of old Eli demanded. But the boys didn't stop there: They seduced Israelite women who came to worship at Shiloh.

Now this was beyond the frozen limit. Sex in a sanctuary was one of the abominations that went on in pagan temples, where female and male prostitutes loitered around the temple porch waiting for customers. For Hophni and Phinehas to introduce such a baldly heathenish practice in a sanctuary holy to the God of Israel was shocking. And since there was no such thing as professional temple prostitutes in Israel, the women targeted by Hophni and Phinehas were decent wives, mothers, and daughters whom the boys either seduced or took by force.

As you'd expect, people complained in the strongest terms to the high priest. So Eli called his sons and asked, "Why do you do these things? For I hear of your evil dealings from all the people. . . . If a man sins against the Lord, who can intercede for him?" It did no good; Hophni and Phinehas turned a deaf ear to their father and went on exploiting the worshippers who came to Shiloh. As for Eli, he gave up trying to reason with his sons—a decision which proved to be a tragic mistake.

Soon after Eli had his useless discussion with his sons, God sent a prophet to Eli with a message that added to the old man's troubles. "Behold, the days are coming," the Lord said through the prophet, "when I will cut off your strength and the strength of your father's house. . . . And this which shall befall your two sons, Hophni and Phinehas, shall be the sign to you: both of them shall die on the same day."

SWINDLERS, NOT SPRINTERS

Some time after Eli received this dreadful prophecy, the men of Israel fought a Philistine army at a place called Ebenezer. On the first day of battle, the Philistines routed the Israelites. Looking for an edge over their enemies when they met again the next day of battle, the Israelites sent a message to the priests at Shiloh, urging them to bring the Ark of the Covenant into the army's camp. The priests who escorted the Ark were none other than Hophni and Phinehas. The army of Israel should have driven the notorious pair from the camp, then sent a message back to Shiloh insisting that truly holy priests escort the Ark. But like Eli, the men of Israel failed in their responsibility to defend what is holy from the manipulation of evil men.

Although the sacred Ark was in the custody of a pair of corrupt, hypocritical priests, its presence in the camp lifted the morale of the Israelites, who cheered in expectation of a great victory over the Philistines. Their exultant shouts echoed across the battlefield to the Philistines' camp, where word was spreading that the Israelites had an edge now that the Ark of the Covenant had come from Shiloh. Some of the Philistines, recalling all they had heard of what the God of Israel had done to the Egyptians, feared that something just as bad or much worse was about to befall them. But other soldiers in the Philistine camp roused their comrades, saying, "Acquit yourselves like men, and fight!"

The next morning the Philistines summoned up their courage and charged across the battlefield. To the Philistines' surprise, the Israelites scattered like sheep. The presence of the Ark did not give the army of Israel a supernatural advantage, and once the Philistine realized this fact, their hearts were filled with joy (not to mention relief). They pursued the fleeing Israelites, slaughtering them by the thousands.

In their desperation to escape the Philistines, no man in the army of Israel gave any thought now to the Ark of the Covenant. The holy object was abandoned with no one to defend it but Hophni and Phinehas. When the two brothers saw a band of fierce, heavily armed Philistine soldiers making straight for the Ark, they panicked and looked for some place to hide; but exposed as they were in the middle of the now deserted Israelite camp, they found no safe refuge, nor were there any Israelite soldiers to protect them. So the brothers hiked up the skirts of their priestly robes and ran. But Hophni and Phinehas were swindlers, not sprinters; the Philistines had no trouble overtaking them, throwing them roughly to the ground, and killing them. Then with a triumphant shout the band of Philistines lifted the

Ark of the Covenant onto their shoulders and carried it back to their camp as a trophy of war.

One of the Israelite soldiers, a man of the tribe of Benjamin, saw the Philistines capture the Ark. Tearing his clothes in grief and casting dirt on his head as a sign of mourning, he ran to Shiloh. Eli, anxious to have the Ark safely back in the sanctuary, had taken a stool outside the city, set it beside the road, and sat down to wait for news. That's where the Benjaminite, bedraggled and out of breath, found the old man. "I am he who has come from the battle," the soldier said. "I fled from the battle today."

Hoping for good news, Eli asked, "How did it go, my son?"

"Israel has fled before the Philistines," the soldier replied, "and there has also been a great slaughter among the people; your two sons, Hophni and Phinehas, are dead, and the Ark of God has been captured."

At that, Eli suffered a violent seizure, fell backwards off his stool, broke his neck and died. Eli was 98 years old.

WHAT HOPHNI AND PHINEHAS
can teach us

YOU'RE THE FATHER—YOU'RE IN CHARGE

Eli was not only Hophni's and Phinehas' father, he was their boss. As high priest he could have ended the scandal easily—by firing the boys, expelling them from the priesthood. That he failed to do so is not a tender example of fatherly love, it is a case of a father who refuses to exercise his authority. Because Eli failed to do his duty as a father and as a high priest, Hophni and Phinehas committed sacrilege in the sanctuary at Shiloh, and exploited the faithful who came to worship there. Perhaps Eli was overly indulgent, perhaps he didn't like confrontation—too bad! He had a responsibility to his sons, to the people of Israel, to the priesthood, and to the Lord. And by letting Hophni and Phinehas have their way, Eli let everyone down.

"Fathers, do not provoke your children to anger, but bring them up in the discipline and instruction of the Lord." (Ephesians 6:4)

TEACH THE KIDS A RELATIVELY EASY LESSON NOW, OR THEY WILL LEARN A TOUGHER LESSON LATER

After showing nothing but contempt for the Lord, Hophni and Phinehas carried the Ark of the Covenant into a battle against the Philistines. Was it a sudden act of faith? Nope. For these two reprobates, the Ark was a magic talisman that would keep them safe and show everyone in both armies that these two guys were "powerful" people that nobody should mess with. For their arrogance, Hophni and Phinehas were struck down in the battle.

As for the army of Israel, every man there knew what scoundrels Hophni and Phinehas were, yet the Israelites still let these two hypocrites profane the sacred Ark. The army's punishment was defeat in battle, and the heartbreak of seeing the Ark carried off by the Philistines as a trophy of war. It was a harsh lesson, but it taught the Israelites (and all the priests of Israel) humility. Once they had learned that lesson, the Ark of the Covenant was restored to them.

"'Yet even now,'" says the Lord, 'return to me with all your heart. . . .'
Return to the Lord, your God, for he is gracious and merciful, slow to
anger, and abounding in steadfast love." (Joel 2:12, 13)

BE FAITHFUL SERVANTS OF THE LORD

The head of a family has lots of responsibilities. If he or she is also the pastor of a church, there are so many additional responsibilities. Yet parents and pastors who strive to set a good example to their children and their congregation, who do their utmost to serve God faithfully and with integrity, will never stray too far from the right path.

"Tend the flock of God that is your charge, not by constraint
but willingly, not for shameful gain but eagerly, not as domineering
over those in your charge but being examples of to the flock.
And when the chief Shepherd is manifested you will obtain
the unfading crown of glory." (1 Peter 5:2–4)

ULTIMATELY, IT WAS A SIN AGAINST LOVE

In his mercy, God placed Hophni and Phinehas in the home of a loving, godly man, but the two boys were ungrateful for this blessing, indifferent to all their father tried to teach them. Willful and arrogant, they got to the point where they did not even attempt to hide their enmity against God and their contempt for everything that is holy. Their outrageous conduct at the Shiloh sanctuary was a flagrant expression of their disdain for God and their rejection of divine law.

"Teacher, what good deed must I do, to have eternal life?. . . If you would enter life, keep the commandments." (Matthew 19:16, 17)

CHAPTER 12

HANUN

BRING IT ON!

2 Samuel 10
2 Samuel 12:26–31

The son of a well-respected king, Hanun had everything going for him. Nevertheless, he failed to appreciate the value of his father's good name and hard work. Upon his father's death, when Hanun became king of the Ammonites, his callous conduct caused more trouble than he bargained for.

Hanun, prince of the Ammonites, was as feckless as any vain child of a successful father. His dad, King Nahash, had been a loyal ally and friend of David, so when the king of the Ammonites died, King David, out of respect and affection for the memory of his friend, sent a delegation to Hanun to console him in his loss and renew the promises of loyalty that existed between the two kingdoms. "I will deal loyally with Hanun the son of Nahash," David said, "as his father dealt loyally with me."

David, of course, had no idea that the new king suffered from an affliction that has troubled many children of famous and successful parents: jealousy stemming from an inability to live up to the accomplishments of their parents. History has shown us many instances of children who, as the offspring of overachieving parents, had a difficult time making peace with the wealth and privileges they inherited, through no efforts of their own. Some manage to cope and make their own way on their own terms. Others, unfortunately, never come to grips with the power that merely bearing a famous name brings. For these children, life must be a curious combination of resentment from living in the shadow of a famous mother or father, along with a sense of entitlement that money and fame bring with them.

Unfortunately, Hanun fell into the second group. In him, we see a young, inexperienced kid who was determined to prove that he could be a better—and more memorable—king than his father.

INSTANT GRATIFICATION

In addition to his other flaws, Hanun was gullible and just a touch paranoid. His advisors, all princes about his own age, all as raw and untested as he was, and each desperate to become the new king's chief counselor, spoon-fed Hanun the kind of nonsense he was all-too-ready to hear. "Do you think, because David has sent comforters to you, that he is honoring your father?" they asked. "Has not David sent his servants to you to search the city, and to spy it out, and to overthrow it?"

These rhetorical questions were a masterstroke, striking Hanun precisely at the spot where he was especially vulnerable: the stability of his throne. By encouraging their king to regard David's emissaries with suspicion, to essentially take the first steps toward alienating a strong ally, Hanun's advisors did their king and their people no favors. It was more than shortsighted: It was suicidal. Wise men think in the long term, but Hanun's advisors were like children, out for instant gratification—in this case, the approval of their king and the rewards that they expected would follow because they told him what he wanted to hear.

AN UNEXPECTED RECEPTION

As a sign of respect for the late King Nahash, David's ambassadors entered Hanun's court dressed in solemn robes. The message they brought from their king was one of sympathy and of friendship. David was pleased to embrace Hanun as an ally. If any nation threatened the Ammonites, Hanun could rely on the Israelites to rush to his aid. And David assumed that if his kingdom came under attack, Hanun would bring his army to defend Israel.

The ambassadors had no chance to deliver their message to the king. They had barely entered his audience hall when Hanun ordered his guards to seize the delegation of Israelites. As the soldiers pinned the stunned ambassadors to the pillars of the hall, barbers stepped forward with razors in their hands. The Israelites thought their throats were about to be cut, but the barbers did not harm King David's ambassadors. They shaved them. It was an odd kind of shave: The barbers shaved only one-half of each man's face, leaving half the beard intact. Then the barbers, still wielding their razors, cut the ambassadors' robes in half, so that the men were naked down to their hips. In this humiliating and shameful condition, the ambassadors were driven from Hanun's palace and into the streets, where they fled from his capital city.

This was a thoroughly satisfying moment for the young king. He had asserted his independence from the precedents set by his father, and from any obligation to David. His reign was off to smashing start.

THE KING'S SYMPATHY

Hanun's conduct toward the ambassadors had far greater significance than simple embarrassment. In the ancient world, a man's beard was a sign of his manhood, a symbol of dignity and of maturity. To shave off a beard was regarded as a symbolic attempt to unman him and reduce him to the status of a boy again. By shaving off only half of each man's beard, Hanun had not only disparaged the manhood of David's delegation of ambassadors, he made them appear ridiculous.

Cutting off half of the ambassadors' clothing was also an assault on their dignity. As emissaries of the king of Israel they deserved to be treated with respect. Instead, Hanun mutilated their best robes and sent them out into the streets half naked, like slaves or the humblest laborers.

These assaults on his ambassadors were an assault on King David. Hanun was issuing a challenge, one which David could not ignore without losing face before the other kings of the Middle East. But David's first concern was for his humiliated emissaries. Word of their mistreatment had reached him, and he sent a message to them: "Remain at Jericho until your beards have grown, and then return." He was not exiling them; he was sparing them the additional shame of having to return to Jerusalem and appear in the royal palace in such an unseemly condition.

THE ODIOUS AMMONITES

Even before David could react to this affront, Hanun realized that his mistreatment of the Israelite ambassadors was essentially a declaration of war. As the author of 2 Samuel says, "The Ammonites saw that they had become odious to David."

That was putting it mildly. Moving quickly, Hanun formed a coalition with three neighboring kings, who put 33,000 men in the field to fight in the impending war against the army of Israel. David sent his best commander, Joab, along with Joab's brother Abishai, to meet the threat. When the two brothers saw the great host arrayed against them, they almost lost their nerve. Almost. "Be of good courage," Joab said to his brother, "and let us play the man for our people, and for the cities of our God, and may the Lord do what seems good to him."

Rather than wait to be attacked, Joab charged. The Ammonites and their allies hadn't expected this. Instead of holding their ground, they turned tail and ran off the battlefield. Chalk one up for the Israelites.

But the Ammonites and their allies were not giving up yet. They rallied, and David found himself engaged in a full-scale war. Alas, he was not quite as involved in the fighting as he otherwise would have been. You see, during the war against Hanun, David spotted Bathsheba bathing on her roof, and you know how that story turned out.

Fortunately for David, while he dallied with Bathsheba, Joab conducted the war, and he did extremely well. Within a year, Joab led the army of Israel against Hanun's capital city, Rabbah, and laid siege to it. This got David's attention. He left Bathsheba and assumed command of the attack on Rabbah. The city fell easily to the Israelites, and Hanun was killed in the fighting. Entering the palace, David found Hanun's body sprawled on the floor, dressed in royal attire. "And he took the crown of [the Ammonites'] king from his head . . . and it was placed on David's head."

The survivors of the battle became the Israelites' slaves. David "set them to labor with saws and iron picks and iron axes, and set them to toil in the brick-kilns; and thus he did to all the cities of the Ammonites."

WHAT HANUN
can teach us

RESPECT THE ACHIEVEMENTS OF YOUR PARENTS

We all know stories of parents who grew up in poverty and never had the advantages of a solid education, but who worked hard so their children could live in nice houses and go to college. All parents (or at least all the good ones) hope and pray that their children will do a little better than they did. It's only right that the children, especially once they become adults, should show their appreciation for all the sacrifices Mom and Dad made for their sake. Hanun took the accomplishments of his father for granted, and, not appreciating the valuable legacy left to him, squandered it in childish pranks that caused immense suffering.

"May you be strengthened with all power, according to his glorious might, for all endurance and patience with joy, giving thanks to the Father, who has qualified us to share in the inheritance of the saints in light." (Colossians 1:11–12)

MIND YOUR MANNERS AND BE
RESPECTFUL OF OTHERS

In ancient times, everyone believed it was an almost sacred obligation to treat guests well. Hanun's disgraceful abuse of David's ambassadors demonstrated to the world that he was not a noble young king, but an ill-mannered brat. Bad manners not only offend your guests, they are a reflection of your character. They paint a picture of you that you may never be able to overcome.

"For the wrongdoer will be paid back for the wrong he has done, and there is no partiality." (Colossians 3:25)

APPRECIATE THE KINDNESSES OF
YOUR NEIGHBORS

It is basic in all societies to offer words of comfort when there has been a death in the family. Even the most grief-stricken can summon up the strength to say "Thank you" to the people who come to the wake or funeral, or make a sympathy call afterward. Yet the churlish Hanun insulted and degraded the men David sent with a message of condolence. By his actions, Hanun proved himself an unworthy king as well as an ungracious and rude neighbor.

"Let each of us please our neighbor for his good, to edify him."
(Romans 15:2)

"So then, as we have opportunity, let us do good to all men, and especially to those who are of the household of faith."
(Galatians 6:10)

MEET CHALLENGES WITH
COURAGE AND FAITH

On the first day of the war against the Ammonite coalition, Joab and Abishai found themselves outnumbered. Putting their trust in the Lord, they attacked their enemies, a show of courage that unnerved the enemy, who scattered like sheep. Like Joab and Abishai, the best way to face hardships is to do whatever it takes to get out of the difficult situation. And also like these two brave men, don't rely entirely on your own efforts—call upon God for help.

"Behold, we call those happy who were steadfast.
You have heard of the steadfastness of Job, and you have
seen the purpose of the Lord, how the Lord is compassionate
and merciful." (James 5:11)

"I know your works, your love and faith and service and
patient endurance, and that your latter works exceed the first."
(Revelation 2:19)

CHAPTER 13

AMNON

THE DEVIL YOU KNOW

2 Samuel 13

If ever a parent needed a guidebook, it was King David. Unfortunately, he didn't have one, and simple things like setting limits, expectations—and a good example—didn't seem to occur to him. So much the worse for three of his many children: Amnon, who couldn't control his sexual passions; Tamar, an innocent victim of Amnon's lust; and Absalom, whose desire for revenge was cold and calculating. If David had better understood what makes a good parent, would these siblings' sad tale have had a different outcome?

King David had at least eight wives with whom he had many children, an unknown number of concubines, and probably the occasional fling. Traditionally we would focus on the tensions and jealousies that would erupt, predictably enough, among the wives and concubines. But in such a large, complicated, extended family, the interaction among all the children was fraught with unpleasantness, too. On top of the usual strain over birth order and the resentments among the girls who must take a back seat to their brothers, all the kids were competing for the attention of their father, the king. If David suddenly favored one wife or one concubine over all the others, that favoritism elevated the status of the woman's children, too. David's palace was not one big, happy family; it was one big, nasty snake pit.

At the top of the heap was David's first-born son, Amnon, the prince who would inherit the crown of Israel. As the future king, he would have been an attractive match for any woman in the kingdom. But Amnon spent no time romancing the young women of Israel: He was obsessed with his half-sister, Tamar. "Amnon was so tormented that he made himself ill because of his sister Tamar," the author of 2 Samuel tells us.

Amnon's conscience was still operational. Nonetheless, he couldn't get those foul thoughts about Tamar out of his head, and the strain began to show. Troubled by dreams of Tamar, Amnon was not sleeping well. During the day he picked at his food. He stopped leaving the palace, which gave him a pallid complexion.

To his credit, Amnon knew that lusting after his sister, even his half-sister, was a vile thing, "for she was a virgin, and it seemed impossible to Amnon to do anything to her." That was a good sign; Amnon's conscience was still operational. Nonetheless, he couldn't get those foul thoughts about Tamar out of his head, and the strain began to show. Troubled by dreams of Tamar, Amnon was not sleeping well. During the day he picked at his food. He stopped leaving the palace, which gave him a pallid complexion. One day his friend and first cousin Jonadab decided to broach the subject. "O son of the king," he said, "why are you so haggard morning after morning?"

Amnon didn't hedge. "I love Tamar, my brother Absalom's sister," he replied.

This was the moment for Jonadab to express shock and horror, and to deliver some sound advice on how Amnon could get such depraved notions out of his head. But like the character Iago in

Shakespeare's tragedy, *Othello*, Jonadab delighted in spreading misery and ruining lives, even within his own family. Instead of helping Amnon get over this unholy desire, Jonadab concocted a scheme so Amnon could possess his half-sister.

"Lie down on your bed, and pretend to be ill," he said, "and when your father comes to see you, say to him, 'Let my sister Tamar come and give me bread to eat, and prepare the food in my sight, that I may see it, and eat it from her hand.'" Amnon, who up until now had been working hard to control his passions, surrendered to Jonadab's suggestion as fast as Eve swallowed the serpent's rationalizations. He slipped off his clothes, climbed into bed, and sent word to his father that he was very ill.

THE HATRED OF AMNON

David had his faults, but he was at heart a loving man, and he had a weakness for his children. He came at once to Amnon's room to see what his sick boy might need. Of course, in Amnon's case this was not about need so much as want. In a feeble voice, barely lifting his head from his pillow and trying to appear as pathetic as possible, Amnon asked for his sister Tamar to come and nurse him. As a royal princess, Tamar did not have many pressing engagements, so David sent his lovely daughter to cook for her poor, sick brother.

With the help of his servants, Amnon managed to get to the kitchen where he watched Tamar as she kneaded dough, forming it into the little heart-shaped dumplings Amnon requested. As Tamar worked, she made cheerful conversation to raise her brother's spirits. But Amnon, wrapped in blankets and sitting in a chair near the oven, was sullen. "He is so weakened by his illness," Tamar thought, "that he cannot even make small talk." Boy, was she wrong. Amnon was trying to determine the perfect moment to drag Tamar to his room and rape her.

When the dumplings were baked to perfection, Tamar pulled the pan from the oven and tipped them out onto a plate. But Amnon, still in a mood, declined to eat with all the servants and attendants watching; to please her brother, Tamar sent them all away.

Then Amnon complained that the heat of the kitchen made him uncomfortable; he wanted to eat in his room. Tamar, a loving sister and a good nurse, indulged him, and helped her brother return to his own chamber. There, once again, she offered him the heart-shaped dumplings he had asked for, holding the plate out to him. Amnon reached out as well, but instead of taking a dumpling, he grabbed Tamar. She struggled to break free from his rough grasp, dropping the plate of dumplings in the process, but Amnon was strong. He held on to Tamar, and, hissing like the serpent in Eden, commanded, "Come, lie with me, my sister."

"No, my brother," the frightened girl replied, "do not force me . . . do not do this wanton folly." But Amnon would not release her, no matter how hard she struggled or begged. Tamar was on the verge of despair, yet she made a desperate effort to outwit her would-be rapist.

"Speak to the king," she suggested, "for he will not withhold me from you." It was a ruse, of course. David would never have tolerated an incestuous marriage in his family, but Tamar hoped that the idea of taking her legitimately would derail Amnon's lust, at least long enough for her to escape from his room. But Amnon had thrown himself over the edge; at this stage no appeal would stop him from committing the crime upon which he had been fixated for so many days. "He would not listen to her; and being stronger than she, he forced her, and lay with her."

The worst sins are the ones we commit when we are fully conscious of how terrible they are. We know that what we are about to do is seriously wrong, and we have an opportunity to stop, yet we do the evil deed anyway.

AMNON: THE DEVIL YOU KNOW

That was Amnon's moral dilemma at that dreadful moment. Bad enough that he was overwhelmed by lust so great that he violently forced his will upon a woman; even more heinous was that the act was committed against his own half-sister. Amnon had become like one of Lucifer's rebel angels, completely and consciously rejecting God and all claims of virtue. He hated what was good, innocent, and pure, and he was intent upon destroying it.

A DESOLATE WOMAN

Once he had possessed Tamar, Amnon was filled with self-loathing. Rather than accept the blame for his actions, he turned his odium against his poor sister. "Amnon hated her with a very great hatred; so that the hatred with which he hated her was greater than the love with which he had loved her." He called his servant and commanded him, "Put this woman out of my presence, and bolt the door after her."

Although she was completely innocent, Tamar was filled with the kind of grief and shame we usually feel when *we've* done something awful. Standing in the street outside her wicked brother's house, she put ashes on her head, tore her fine robe, covered her face with her hands. Weeping loudly, she hurried to the home of her brother Absalom. There, "Tamar dwelt, a desolate woman."

Word of the incestuous rape enraged David, but he did nothing to punish Amnon. As for Absalom, he "spoke to Amnon neither good nor bad." From Amnon's point of view, he'd gotten away with it.

David's inaction after one of his daughters has been raped by one of his sons is inexcusable. Amnon had broken the laws of God and man, he had brought trouble and pain on his own family, yet David did not even reprimand him. No wonder Tamar felt desolate. Her brother had assaulted her, dishonored her, and according to the mores of the day ruined her chances of ever marrying. In the aftermath of the rape, her own father did nothing to avenge her or punish Amnon.

Absalom's lack of reaction to the rape of his sister by his brother must have struck many observers as odd, too. But as we will see, he was a boy with a plan.

UNFINISHED BUSINESS

Two years later, Tamar's rape was a painful memory of which no one in the royal family spoke. When the season of shearing the sheep came around again, Absalom invited his father and all his brothers and half-brothers to his home for a feast. David begged off, saying that hosting so many guests would be burdensome to Absalom, but the prince insisted that at least all the princes should come. In the end, enticed by the promise of fine food and an endless flow of wine, the sons of David all said they would be delighted to attend Absalom's banquet. Amnon promised he would come, too.

Absalom's plans were extremely precise and detailed; he wanted everything to go exactly as he had planned. As the day of the feast approached, he met with his servants to go over the final details, giving them one last set of orders. "Mark when Amnon's heart is merry with wine," he said, "and when I say, 'Strike Amnon,' then kill him." The princes' cousin Jonadab had been crafty, but Absalom combined cunning with patience. Two years had gone by and no harm had come to Amnon; now, when his guard was down, Absalom would avenge Tamar.

The princes drank wine as they watched the shepherds shear the sheep. They drank wine as they waited for dinner to be announced. Reclining on their couches in Absalom's banquet room, they drank yet more wine as the servants brought in tray after tray of rich food.

By now, the hearts of all the sons of David were merry with wine—all except Absalom. He had remained stone cold sober throughout the party. As the conversations became louder and the laughter more raucous, Absalom beckoned to his steward, the man who ran Absalom's household. The steward leaned close as his master whispered in his ear, "Strike Amnon."

Rising, the steward caught the eyes of the servants in the room. Moving quickly and stealthily, they moved from their places and gathered behind Amnon's couch. Amnon, giddy from wine and laughter, did not notice, even as the servants drew sharp daggers from beneath their robes. Then, the servants closed in on the drunken prince, stabbing him repeatedly, ignoring his cries of shock and pain. After a moment, they stepped back, then turned and hurried from the banquet room.

As the other revelers began to realize what had happened, the laughter and chatter that had so recently filled the room faded to a terrible silence. The celebrants stared, immobilized by terror, as Amnon, bloody and gasping for life, rolled off his couch and fell to the floor, dead. Then, with cries of fear and horror, tripping over each other and the furniture as they gathered themselves and ran, Absalom's brothers and half-brothers rushed from the house to the safety of the palace of their father, David.

As the other revelers began to realize what had happened, the laughter and chatter that had so recently filled the room faded to a terrible silence. The celebrants stared, immobilized by terror, as Amnon, bloody and gasping for life, rolled off his couch and fell to the floor, dead.

BAD KIDS OF THE BIBLE

In the banquet room, no one remained but Absalom and the body of Amnon. Standing over the corpse, Absalom smiled with satisfaction, then commanded his servants to pack his bags. That same day Absalom went to stay with his grandfather, King Talmai, in his kingdom of Geshur in what is now southwestern Syria.

The news that Absalom had left the kingdom broke David's heart, and he mourned the departure of his handsome son. But David wasted no tears on Amnon. What mixed messages David sent to his children! Amnon had raped Tamar, but the king did not lift a finger to defend his daughter or punish his son. Then, Absalom murdered Amnon, and David shed tears—not for the murdered Amnon, but for Absalom who had run away from home. Note that while Scripture praises David as a man after the Lord's own heart, as a great king, as a brilliant poet and talented musician, even as a good dancer, at no point does Scripture suggest that David was Father of the Year.

WHAT AMNON
can teach us

KEEP SEXUAL PASSIONS IN CHECK—AND SEXUAL BEHAVIOR APPROPRIATE

Contemporary society is often described as sex-obsessed, and there is something to that description. But distorted ideas about sexuality are not new, and the sad history of violent assaults against women is older than the Bible. Amnon's single-minded focus on self-gratification reduced his half-sister Tamar to an object that he could use, then toss aside when his needs had been met.

Unlike Amnon, most men are not rapists, and fewer still would contemplate so terrible a crime against a sister. Even so, there is a big gap between the brutality Amnon evidenced and normal sexual expression. In your intimate encounters with your spouse, remember that love, respect, and consideration are what transform the act of sex into an act of love.

"For we ourselves were once foolish, disobedient, led astray, slaves to various passions and pleasures, passing our days in malice and envy, hated by men and hating one another, but when the goodness and loving kindness of God our Savior appeared, he saved us, not because of deeds done by us in righteousness, but in virtue of his own mercy." (Titus 3:3–5)

INJUSTICE WILL NOT LAST FOREVER

How often have you felt like Tamar, wronged by others yet sitting o n the sidelines incredulous as the wicked run amok in the world and no one even censures them let alone tries to stop them? It's easy to believe (wrongly) that God isn't paying attention. But He is.

"Let God arise, let his enemies be scattered; let those who hate him flee before him! . . . Father of the fatherless and protector of widows is God in his holy habitation. God gives the desolate a home to dwell in; he leads out the prisoners to prosperity." (Psalm 68:1, 5–6)

MAN'S RETALIATION DOES NOT EQUAL GOD'S JUSTICE

The rape of his sister and his father's unwillingness to do a thing about it brought out the worst in Absalom. We can understand his rage, his craving for pay back, but he had neither the right nor the authority to punish Amnon. What Amnon did was evil, inexcusable. But what Absalom did was evil and inexcusable, too, even if our instincts might try to convince us that Absalom's actions were at least understandable.

No doubt, Absalom told himself that it was justice he was after. He was deluding himself, of course; what he wanted was simple retaliation. He did not arraign Amnon before a court; he ambushed him in his own home. By his actions, Absalom did not blot out Amnon's crime. He just added a new crime—and a new misery—to the pile.

In our own lives, we may fantasize about taking justice into our own hands. Let such thoughts remain fantasies, or better yet get them out of your head. Maybe it's as simple as "Two wrongs don't make a right."

"Let love be genuine; hate what is evil, hold fast to what is good."
(Romans 12:9)

"Vengeance is mine, I will repay, says the Lord." (Romans 12:19)

AS A PARENT, BE A LEADER, NOT A PAL

As king, David was a father figure to the people of Israel. But he was also a biological father, the parent of a large family. Both types of fatherhood required that David set a good example. But the story of Amnon, Tamar, and Absalom teaches us a lesson about how a father ought *never* to act, either as leader of a people or as head of a household.

It's hard to know why David, as a father, set so lax an example and tolerated such brutish behavior. Perhaps he feared that if he laid down the law, his children wouldn't like him any more. Maybe it was more important to him to be a pal. Sometimes, too, beleaguered and overworked parents may feel it's easier just to give up and give in rather than stand up to a child's demands and tantrums. What happened in this story is extreme, of course; not all lax parenting leads to such horrific deeds. But David had an obligation to set an example of striving to do what was right, and resisting, even punishing, what was wrong. He dropped the ball, with tragic consequences for his children—and for himself.

"You are the light of the world. A city set on a hill cannot be hid. Nor do men light a lamp and place it under a bushel, but on a stand, and it gives light to all in the house. Let your light so shine before men, that they may see your good works and give glory to your Father who is in heaven." (Matthew 5:14–16)

FOR GOOD OR BAD, WE ALWAYS HAVE A CHOICE IN HOW WE ACT

In times of great temptation, there is always a moment when we choose our course—to draw back and cling to what we know is right and good, or to take the dive into the abyss that we think will satisfy our desires and make us happy. Amnon had been struggling on the edge of that abyss, and he had a decent shot at overcoming his evil desires until Jonadab showed up. Before he dragged poor Tamar to his bed, Amnon had already committed the sins of deception, manipulation, and betrayal. With Jonadab's prodding and help, he lied and exploited his father's and sister's natural feelings of love and compassion.

Amnon allowed himself to be influenced for bad, in spite of what he knew to be right. That was his choice, and it brought shame and grief to so many others. The choices we're faced with may not be as serious, but they may still have the power to bring a measure of happiness or sadness to ourselves and others. Can we choose for the good, whatever the temptation?

"Since all have sinned and fall short of the glory of God, they are justified by his grace as a gift, through the redemption which is in Christ Jesus." (Romans 3:23–24)

CHAPTER 14

ABSALOM

REVERSAL OF FORTUNE

2 Samuel 14

Absalom, the son of a king, had everything going for him—position, money, good looks, a charming personality. But he chose to squander it all, giving in to an egomaniacal and rebellious spirit that led him to dishonor and even try to destroy his own father. Just when it seemed that Absalom's evil, shameless cunning might triumph, his world was tragically undone by a seemingly harmless symbol of his vanity.

Absalom, the third-born son of King David of Israel, could have been one of those over-achieving kids who takes first prize at the school science fair, wins the state spelling bee, does a little options trading online before supper, and is captain of the varsity track team. But arrogance, selfishness, and vanity distorted his natural talents; the fact that he was slated to succeed his father as king only intensified Absalom's self-absorption. His family would tolerate him at holidays and family parties, but otherwise preferred to keep him at arm's length. The ordinary men and women of Israel, however, were taken in by his charm, his common touch, and his movie-star good looks complete with luxuriant flowing hair and dazzling smile.

"Now in all Israel there was no one so much to be praised for his beauty as Absalom; from the sole of his foot to the crown of his head there was no blemish in him."

Given the dysfunctional nature of the family, though, Absalom's personality faults aren't surprising. David had many wives and concubines, and the family history was riddled with episodes of greed, corruption, even murder. The dysfunction reached crisis-level after Amnon, David's eldest son and Absalom's half-brother, raped their sister Tamar. How David and Absalom reacted to this horror created a father-son standoff that lasted for years. David did not punish Amnon for assaulting Tamar, which Absalom would not forgive; in retaliation, Absalom lured Amnon to his house and killed him, which David would not forgive.

After the murder, Absalom fled. For three years, he stayed at his grandfather's palace in Geshur. Absalom saw this act as keeping a safe distance between himself and his irrational father; David saw it as a cowardly son hiding behind an old man. But three years is a long time, long enough for a sentimental man like David to mellow—to a degree. He sent a message to his father-in-law in Geshur, saying that Absalom could return to Jerusalem. The catch was that Absalom could have no contact with David.

David's action was more than the sentimental gesture of an indulgent father, however: He needed to have Absalom back. After the murder of Amnon, David's second eldest son, Daniel, had died, leaving Absalom as the crown prince and heir to the throne. Like any good king, David recognized that the future of his dynasty was more important than a family squabble, but just because he had to let Absalom return to Jerusalem didn't mean he had to socialize with him.

David was caught in the dilemma that many parents face when a child has done something dreadful. He loved Absalom, he wanted to reconcile with him, but Absalom showed no signs of remorse. He was not sorry that he had killed Amnon, nor was he sorry that he had wounded his father's feelings. And so David took a "tough love" approach—where there is no repentance, there can be no forgiveness.

PLAYING THE PALACE

Absalom, however, was in no mood to repent. While he was away in Geshur, his innate selfishness had intensified, and David's approach simply irritated him. Although Absalom had stifled any love he once had for David, like a petulant child, he still wanted David to love him. Irrational, yes, but logic had never been Absalom's forte.

Absalom took a new approach. If David's most trusted general, Joab, interceded for him, Absalom reasoned, the king would relent and invite Absalom to the palace. Twice Absalom appealed to Joab; both times the general ignored the prince. In a fit of pique, Absalom sent his servants to one of Joab's fields where the barley was ripening. "Set it on fire," Absalom commanded, and the servants obeyed.

That got Joab's attention. Before the smoke had cleared from his blackened field, Joab went to Absalom's house. Absalom didn't waste time with apologies. He wanted to see his father, and he wanted Joab to smooth the way. Like the other members of the royal household, the general couldn't stand the prince, but he didn't want all of his crops ruined either, so he agreed to serve as mediator and persuade the king. Urged on by Joab, David did relent and invite his prodigal son to the palace.

On the appointed day, Absalom entered his father's throne room, where he prostrated himself before his father. A few common people of Israel who were in the hall that day were moved to tears by the sight of their handsome prince, face-down on the palace floor, begging for forgiveness. The members of the court, who knew Absalom, rolled their eyes as they observed yet another melodramatic, "look-at-me!" moment. But David, who was always a soft touch where his children were concerned, rose, came down the steps, lifted his son off the floor, and kissed him. Once again, Absalom had gotten exactly what he wanted. And once again, it wasn't enough.

No, for Absalom it was not enough to be loved, to be forgiven, to be welcomed home with open arms, to be assured that all the nastiness of the past had been buried and forgotten. That was all a distant second to *winning*. The thing the prince wanted was for the royal family to come to him, en masse, and say, "Gee, we never should have been upset when you killed your brother without ever appealing for justice from the king, the courts, or any other representative of the law. It was so wrong-headed of us to think that cold-blooded murder is bad."

No, for Absalom it was not enough to be loved,
to be forgiven, to be welcomed home with open arms,
to be assured that all the nastiness of the past had been
buried and forgotten. That was all a distant
second to winning.

A JUDGE IN THE LAND,
A TRAITOR IN THE PALACE

Once he was back in his father's favor, Absalom's self-destructive tendencies reemerged and he began undermining his relationship with David. In the most ostentatious and attention-grabbing action ever described in the Bible, Absalom bought a chariot and a team of fine horses, and recruited fifty virile guys to run ahead of his chariot whenever he drove through the streets. Absalom also started to rise with the sun, then hurry out to the palace gate where he confronted everyone who had come to present a personal petition to the king. After listening to the supplicant's story, Absalom would sigh, shake his head, and say, "Your claims are good and right, but there is no man deputed by the king to hear you." While the poor men and women tried to absorb the shock that King David wouldn't lift a finger to help them, Absalom would look up to heaven and cry, "Oh that

I were judge in the land! Then every man with a suit or cause might come to me and I would give him justice."

The people of Israel were taken in and deeply moved that their handsome, sympathetic prince would side with them against his own father. Whenever Absalom appeared in the streets of Jerusalem, he was mobbed by enthusiastic crowds who jostled each other to touch his robe or kiss his hands. The more they loved Absalom, the less they loved King David.

"So Absalom stole the hearts of the men of Israel."

It took time for Absalom to build up his power base in Israel, but after four years he was ready. The Israelites, who had been completely hoodwinked by his charm, could hardly wait for the prince to become king. Yet all the while that Absalom schemed, David remained clueless.

Absalom chose Hebron as the place where he would launch his coup against his father. It was his birthplace as well as the site of David's original capital before he moved to Jerusalem. It was also a holy place, the location of the Tomb of the Patriarchs, where Abraham and Sarah, Isaac and Rebecca, and Jacob and Leah were buried. When Absalom mentioned to his father that he would like to travel to Hebron to offer sacrifice to the Lord, David, ever unsuspecting, gave his son his blessing. Meanwhile, Absalom had sent runners to every corner of the kingdom to deliver a single message: When the people heard the trumpets sound, they were all to shout, "Absalom is king at Hebron!"

With an escort of two hundred men, Absalom traveled to Hebron. There, he offered sacrifice, then waited for his throng of followers to arrive. And they came—so many that when word of the rebellion reached David, the king panicked and abandoned Jerusalem, leaving only ten of his concubines in the palace "to keep the house," as Scripture puts it. Zadok the priest intended to join his king in exile, and he brought with him the sacred Ark of the Covenant, but David insisted that Zadok go back and return the Ark to its sanctuary in the city.

Then the king, barefoot and weeping as if he were the penitent, fled his capital by way of the Mount of Olives. At the summit, he ran into one of his counselors, Hushai, who also was ready to follow his king into exile. By this time, however, David's composure was beginning to return. He urged Hushai to go back to Jerusalem and confer with Zadok. Together they were to convince Absalom that they were his loyal servants now. As Absalom grew to trust the men, as his ego would surely lead him to do, and reveal his plans to them, they would pass the information along to David.

By now, the scales had fallen from David's eyes and he realized the truth about Absalom: His beloved son was nothing more than a treacherous little weasel. To preserve his kingdom and the peace and security of the people of Israel, as well as his own life and the lives of all his family and supporters, David would have to be as cagey as he had been years earlier when King Saul had sought to kill him. It was a challenging moment for David the king, and a tragic, heart-wrenching one for David the father.

SHORT-LIVED GLORY

Absalom's entrance into Jerusalem was a triumphal procession, with an immense host of the people of Israel cheering him as he passed into the capital. As the procession drew near the palace, Hushai emerged from the crowd, shouting, "Long live the king! Long live the king!" These were words Absalom loved to hear, but the fact they came from one of his father's most trusted counselors made the prince suspicious.

"Why did you not go with your friend?" the prince asked. But Hushai had not spent years as a diplomat for nothing.

"Whom the Lord and all this people and all the men of Israel have chosen," he replied, "his I will be, and with him I will remain." Flattery always worked with Absalom. He made Hushai part of his inner circle of friends and advisors.

Now that he was king, Absalom was uncertain what to do next. Fortunately, he had his father's chief counselor, Ahithophel, to teach him. As a public expression of his right to David's throne and to everything else that had been David's, Ahithophel urged Absalom to have sex with the ten concubines David had left behind in the palace. For the orgy, Ahithophel built a pavilion on top of the palace roof where "Absalom went in to his father's concubines in the sight of all Israel."

This was a shameless act, intended to assert Absalom's power, to demonstrate to the people that David could not even protect the women of his household, let alone an entire nation. The fact that the prince would do such a thing in public, where people passing in the street could see him, tells us that Absalom had lost all sense of decency and tossed aside traditional notions of respect and self-restraint.

Absalom's triumph was short lived. David still knew how to raise an army, and a few days after Absalom's coup d'etat, David's men and Absalom's followers met in the forest of Ephraim. Fighting in this wilderness was hard, and at the end of the day twenty thousand men lay dead. But the victory belonged to David.

DUCK!

When Absalom saw that he had been defeated, he jumped on his mule and rode into the forest to escape. As the mule dashed beneath the low hanging limbs of a giant oak tree, Absalom's long flowing hair became entangled in the branches. Just like that, Absalom was jerked off the frantic mule, who kept running, leaving the prince dangling helplessly by his hair from the tree.

One of David's men saw the mishap and carried word of it to the king's general, Joab. The general had never forgiven Absalom for burning his field of grain, and the prince's coup against King David had endeared him even less to Joab. Gathering up three spears and collecting an entourage of ten men, Joab rode hard for the forest. There he found Absalom, still suspended by his hair, arms flailing, legs kicking, trying desperately to free himself.

Drawing up his horse, Joab trotted up to the helpless Absalom. Without a word he drew out one spear and skewered the prince, then thrust the last two into Absalom's heart. Joab's escort hacked at Absalom's body while it still hung from the tree. Absalom, the handsome and privileged prince who had received so many blessings that he did not recognize, was cut down from the branch by Joab's men, his mutilated corpse tossed into a pit and covered with rocks.

It was a soldier from Cush, a place in what is now northern Sudan, who brought news of the death of Absalom to David. The Cushite considered himself a lucky man because, by tradition, a courier who brought good news from the battlefield received lavish gifts from the king. But to the Cushite's astonishment, David did not rejoice. Instead he collapsed in tears, repeating over and over, "O my son Absalom, my son, my son Absalom! Would I had died instead of you, O Absalom, my son, my son!"

WHAT ABSALOM
can teach us

PRIDE GOES BEFORE A FALL

When Absalom looked in the mirror he saw a fine figure of a man. When he listened to himself speak he heard a charismatic guy who could schmooze the entire people of Israel. If he had spent half as much time examining his heart, his soul, his actions, and his motives as he spent grooming his hair, his story would have had a happy ending. But the boy was self-mesmerized—the sun rose and set on Absalom. And if he felt the touch of God's grace, he resisted it.

"God opposes the proud, but gives grace to the humble." (James 4:6)

BEAUTY IS ONLY SKIN DEEP

The ancient Greeks had a story about a beautiful young man named Narcissus who saw his own reflection in the surface of deep pool, became infatuated, tried to embrace the reflection, fell into the pool, and sank to the bottom like a stone. By this we see that even pagans understand the futility of personal vanity. First of all, physical beauty withers with age. Diet, exercise, even cosmetic surgery will never restore the bloom and vitality of youth. But a beautiful soul is forever young, and pleasing to the Lord. And, tragically, a beautiful soul was the one attribute Absalom didn't care about at all.

"For all is vanity, and striving after wind." (Ecclesiastes 2:7)

NOTHING IS MORE PAINFUL
THAN A WAYWARD CHILD

Many families know the sorrow of having a hostile, rebellious child who will not be curbed. Yet even when the kid is a monster, Mom and Dad still hold out hope that he will turn his life around and come back to them. God feels the same way about us, His children. When the kingdom of Ephraim, the ten northern tribes of Israel, rejected the Lord to worship pagan gods, He said to His prophet Jeremiah, "My heart still yearns for him." (Jeremiah 31:20)

The parable of the Prodigal Son illustrates vividly the joy of a father when his wayward boy repents. And of course, as John's gospel tells us, Jesus "came to His own, and His own received him not." (John 1:11) If such a situation exists in your family, pray that God will grant you patience and your child wisdom to at long last accept the Lord's grace, come home, and start anew.

"My son, keep your father's commandment,
and forsake not your mother's teaching. Bind them upon
your heart always." (Proverbs 6:20–21)

GOD'S PATIENCE WITH A PERSISTENT SINNER HAS LIMITS

You can read the story of Absalom as an allegory, with David representing God, and Absalom an obstinate sinner. God loves the sinner and waits patiently for the day he will come to his senses and feel real sorrow for sins and ask forgiveness. The sinner, however, blinded by pride, will not give in. The longer the sinner persists in his pride, the harder his heart becomes and the less receptive he is to God's grace. And such an unhappy situation can have unpleasant eternal repercussions.

> *"He knows every deed of man. He has not commanded any one to be ungodly, and he has not given any one permission to sin. . . . As great as his mercy, so great is also his reproof." (Sirach 15:19–20, 16:12)*

COUNT YOUR BLESSINGS

The sad story of Absalom is the story of a young man who was blessed with wealth, position, good looks, and charisma, but who grossly misused these gifts to advance himself at the expense even of his own father. Rather than feeling humble and grateful for the many blessings God had showered upon him, Absalom was puffed up with hubris—the word the ancient Greeks used to describe a degree of pride so excessive that it offended heaven.

The real tragedy of Absalom's story, however, is his failure to apologize to his father for all the pain and trouble he had caused. David, who knew from first-hand experience the vital importance of atoning for grievous sins (remember the Bathsheba and Uriah debacle?), would have forgiven Absalom. God would have forgiven him, too.

"Create in me a clean heart, O God, and put a new
and right spirit within me. . . . Restore to me the joy of thy salvation."
(Psalm 51: 10, 12)

"Seek the Lord, all you humble of the land, who do his
commands; seek righteousness, seek humility."
(Zephaniah 2:3)

CHAPTER 15

SHEBA

KING FOR A DAY, FOOL FOR A LIFETIME

2 Samuel 20

As a child, Sheba was miserable. It seemed to him that the things he wanted, he was not entitled to have. He didn't grow out of this unfortunate mindset as a young man, either, when his envy of King David prompted him to make a grab for the throne. With no regard for the enormous pain and suffering he was about to inflict on so many innocent people, Sheba pursued his unholy goal...until an old woman stopped him dead in his tracks.

Every playground has a kid who wants to choose all the games everyone plays and make all the rules. This could be an early sign of stellar leadership qualities and organizational skills that will blossom later. On the other hand, the kid may be bossy, authoritarian, obsessed with dominating everyone else. No good comes from that kind of aggressive behavior.

As a boy Sheba, discovered it was smarter and more effective to be cunning rather than violent. He could have become the village bully, lashing out at his targets and terrorizing them, but instead little Sheba observed what was happening around him, used that information to manipulate his playmates and in this way, in the end, he got whatever it was he wanted.

At the root of rebellion is the refusal to obey authority. Some rebellions arise to correct injustice, or overthrow a tyrant. Other rebellions are a grab for power. The author of 2 Samuel tells us that by the time Sheba, the son of Bichri, was a young man he was already "a worthless fellow" who had stirred up his neighbors to revolt against King David. Sheba and his rebels were Benjaminites, a tribe that had remained loyal to King Saul, and lamented that the crown had passed out of Saul's family to David. But when Sheba blew his trumpet to attract the attention of his neighbors, and called on them to rise up against David, he did not suggest tracking down some distant relation of Saul and placing him on the throne (you will remember that all the sons of Saul had died with their father in battle against the Philistines at Gilboa, but one of Saul's cousins or nephews was probably still around). In his heart, Sheba was planning to make himself king of Israel.

ON THE BRINK OF THE ABYSS

Sheba may have been a worthless fellow, but he must have had some appeal, because the Benjaminites followed him willingly. And while there is no arguing that he schemed to overthrow David and seize the throne, Sheba had the good sense to mask his ambition. But David realized that Sheba was a serious threat. In a conversation with one of his commanders, Abishai, David said, "Sheba the son of Bichri will do us more harm than Absalom." And the king's assessment was correct, because by that time the rebellion had spread beyond the tribe of Benjamin; now Sheba was in command of "all the men of Israel," meaning the ten northern tribes. That left David with the two southern tribes of Judah. Although all the men of Judah "followed their king steadfastly," they were grossly outnumbered.

Sheba's timing was excellent. David had barely recovered the from Absalom's rebellion. In fact, the king had only recently reconciled with Absalom's commander, Amasa. To placate any surviving supporters of Absalom, David made Amasa his general. A second revolt, coming on the heels of Absalom's, would make David appear weak. There were still rebels in the land and probably in the court, too. Now that one of Absalom's most trusted advisors was in command of

David's army, there was an excellent chance that all the troops would rally to Sheba if it appeared that he had broad support among the Israelites. David stood teetering on the brink of an abyss, and Sheba was itching to shove him off the edge.

SEALED WITH A KISS

As a rebel, there was a virtue Sheba did not understand: loyalty. And David had loyal people around him: the men of Judah, of course, but also the brothers, Joab and Abishai, two of the finest officers in the royal army. Joab especially was unswervingly loyal to David, even if he did demonstrate his fierce allegiance in violent ways. It was Joab, you'll recall, who drove three spears into Absalom's treacherous heart as the young prince dangled by his hair in the branches of the oak tree. Another revolt against David coming so soon after Absalom's attempted coup enraged Joab. Of course, losing his position as commander of David's army to that traitor, Amasa, did nothing to calm Joab's turbulent temperament.

Faithful as ever to their king, Joab and Abishai assembled an army, "all mighty men," to fight for David. Then they marched to Gibeon, where they would rendezvous with Amasa and pursue Sheba. Near a great stone that was a famous landmark at Gibeon, Amasa stood waiting to greet Joab and Abishai. On seeing Amasa, Joab dismounted. He was wearing a long military cloak, and clutched in his left hand beneath his cloak was his sword. When he reached Amasa, Joab said, "Is it well with you, my brother?" Then seizing Amasa's beard with his right hand, he leaned forward as if he were about to kiss him. Amasa leaned forward to receive the kiss, and as he did so, Joab thrust his sword deep into Amasa's stomach. It was a fatal wound, so Joab did not bother to strike again.

As "Amasa lay wallowing in his blood on the highway," a soldier of Joab stood over the body and proclaimed, "Whoever favors Joab, and whoever is for David, let him follow Joab." The sight of their late commander's corpse made some of the troops uneasy, so the soldier carried Amasa's body into a field where he laid it down and covered it with a garment. No longer obliged to step over Amasa's dead body in order to support David, the army rallied and set out to find Sheba.

JOAB'S SECRET WEAPON

Sheba needed a stronghold for his base of operations, a command center where he could plan his overthrow of David. He chose a walled city in the northernmost region of Israel, Abel of Bethmaacah. The town overlooked the headwaters of the River Jordan, and stood amidst lush, lovely farmland. Far from David's capital city of Jerusalem, well defended and with plenty of food and water to supply the army, Abel of Bethmaacah was everything Sheba required in a citadel. But the rebels had barely settled in when David's army, under the command of Joab and Abishai, arrived outside the walls. Sheba ordered the gates barred and sent his men to the battlements, but the king's army did not attack. The walls of Abel of Bethmaacah were too strong; no army could storm the city. Instead, Joab and Abishai surrounded Abel of Bethmaacah so that no one inside could escape. Then the troops began constructing a huge earthen mound against a portion of the ramparts. Once the mound was finished, a detachment of Joab's soldiers rolled up a massive log battering ram and began pounding the wall.

The rhythmic sound of the log against the stone walls echoed down the streets of Abel of Bethmaacah, unnerving Sheba's soldiers and frightening the civilians. It was only a matter of time before the mortar would crack and the stones give way, letting David's army pour through the breach in the walls to massacre Sheba and his rebels as well as all the inhabitants of the town that gave him shelter.

THE PROBLEM-SOLVER OF ABEL

Above the dreadful sound of the battering ram striking the city wall, Joab's soldiers heard a woman's voice crying, "Hear! Hear!" Looking up, they saw an elderly woman standing on the battlements above their heads, waving her arms and shouting to be heard above the din of the battering ram. Seeing that she had gotten the soldiers' attention at last, the woman cried, "Tell Joab, 'Come here, that I may speak to you.'" It was an odd request. What would an old woman have to say to the general? But one of the soldiers ran off with the message.

To the surprise of the men at the battering ram, Joab came. Scurrying up the earthen mound, he halted the ram so he could hear the woman clearly. But she wanted to be reassured before she said anything. "Are you Joab?" she asked. "I am," the general replied. "Listen to the word of your maidservant," the woman said. "They were wont to say in old time, 'Let them but ask counsel in Abel'; and so they settled a matter. I am one of those who are peaceable and faithful in Israel; you seek to destroy a city which is a mother in Israel; why will you swallow up the heritage of the Lord?"

"Far be it from me, far be it," Joab replied, "that I should swallow up or destroy! That is not true. But a man of the hill country of Ephraim, called Sheba the son of Bichri, has lifted up his hand against King David; give him up alone, and I will withdraw from the city."

The woman did not ask for a moment to consider Joab's proposition. She shouted back, "Behold, his head shall be thrown to you over the wall."

The author of 2 Samuel describes this unnamed woman as "wise." Clearly she was also gutsy, not to mention pragmatic. You might even say she was a first-rate problem-solver.

THE COUNTERREVOLUTION

Scared off by the pounding of the battering ram, unwilling to be the first to die when the men of Judah stormed into the city, the rebel troops had deserted this portion of the ramparts. Consequently, none of Sheba's men heard the woman and Joab negotiate a reprieve for the city.

While Joab waited on the mound, the woman slipped from house to house, telling her neighbors of the deal she had made with Joab. Relieved that they could save their necks after all, the people of Abel of Bethmaacah rose up in a huge mob and ran for the house in which Sheba had made his headquarters. They broke down the doors, and rampaged through the rooms until they found Sheba alone: At the outset of this uprising in the city, all of his officers and men had deserted him. The mob surged into the room, backing the young rebel against a wall where they stabbed him to death. Then they cut off his head.

Outside the city, Joab could hear the tumult in the streets. The counterrevolution, led by the wise woman, had begun. In a little while the woman reappeared on the battlements. Without saying a word, she drew back her arms and hurled an object over the walls. Sheba's severed head landed at Joab's feet, bounced, then rolled down the slope of the mound.

Joab kept his part of the bargain, too. He abandoned the battering ram, lifted the siege, dispersed his troops, and rode back to Jerusalem to bring David the news that the rebellion was over and Sheba, the son of Bichri, was dead.

SHEBA: KING FOR A DAY, FOOL FOR A LIFETIME

WHAT SHEBA
can teach us

THERE'S A REASON WHY ENVY IS LISTED AMONG THE SEVEN DEADLY SINS

There is a difference between the sin of envy and a healthy sense of competition. A competitive person looks upon the success and happiness of another and tries to imitate what he or she did to achieve it. There's nothing wrong about that—in fact, it's laudable. But if the success and happiness of another causes you pain, you are up to your eyebrows in envy.

With the defeat of Absalom, King David had escaped exile and perhaps death, yet Sheba was not happy for the king. Instead, Sheba coveted the crown for himself and pursued unjust means to become king.

"Do not lay up for yourselves treasures on earth, where moth and rust consume and where thieves break in and steal, but lay up for yourselves treasures in heaven, where neither moth nor rust consumes and where thieves do not break in and steal. For where your treasure is, there will your heart be also." (Matthew 6:19–21)

DISCONTENTED PEOPLE CAN CAUSE SO MUCH TROUBLE

Children aren't the only ones who have a fit when they don't get their own way. Lots of adults are still locked into that pattern (hence, the expression, "My way or the highway"). God handpicked David—not Sheba—to be king of Israel. Rather than submit to the will of the Lord, Sheba rebelled, seized what did not belong to him, started a civil war, and almost brought about the massacre of every man, woman, and child in the town of Abel.

"Better a little with righteousness than great revenues with injustice."
(Proverbs 16:8)

FAITHFULNESS IS REWARDED

Faithfulness to God and to our obligations in this world is the express lane to happiness. It curbs our pride and our passions, reduces selfishness, gets us into the habit of using the law of God as the benchmark for our actions, draws us closer to the Lord, and helps us to acquire the other virtues Paul listed in his letter to the Galatians.

"But the fruit of the Spirit is love, joy, peace, patience, kindness, goodness, faithfulness, gentleness, self-control."
(Galatians 5:22–23)

CHAPTER 16

ADONIJAH

THE BOY WHO WOULD BE KING

1 Kings 1

Adonijah repeated the same mistakes as his older brother Absalom. Vain and self-centered, Adonijah decided to push his claim to succeed his father, David, as king—and he didn't care what he had to do to get what he wanted. But dividing and conquering doesn't always work, as Adonijah discovered when King David nipped his plan in the bud.

David had many fine qualities, but he was not the world's most decisive father. By his many wives he had many sons, yet he was coy about which prince would succeed him as king of Israel. He had made a promise to Bathsheba that their son, Solomon, despite the fact that he was not one of the eldest boys, would inherit the throne, but David hadn't told anyone else, and Bathsheba had kept quiet about their plan, too.

Princes don't have much to do. The only one who has a "job" is the heir, who sits around patiently waiting for his father to die. The princes who will not be king spend their days and nights hunting, feasting, and chasing peasant girls. But the motivated princes indulge in a bit of scheming. Adonijah was one of these highly motivated princes.

Now that his older brothers, Amnon and Absalom, were dead, Adonijah figured that he was David's heir. This was heady stuff for a boy who all his life had been third in line for the throne. Of course, there was no way anyone could have predicted that Amnon would rape their sister, Tamar, and Absalom would kill him; or that Absalom would try to overthrow David, and Joab would kill him. Nonetheless, here Adonijah was, the obvious choice as next king of Israel.

While the other princes had grown up to be frivolous young men, Adonijah had a just appreciation of his qualities, and he knew how to use them. As a little boy people had been drawn to him because he was so beautiful—just like his big brother, Absalom. But if he threw a tantrum, or whined, or lashed out at other children, those adults who had found him so attractive because of his angelic appearance would leave him (except his mother and his nurse, of course, who were stuck with little Adonijah). So Adonijah learned to be nice, or at least appear to be nice. He discovered that a pleasant disposition combined with natural good looks could win people over every time.

While the other princes had grown up to be frivolous young men, Adonijah had a just appreciation of his qualities, and he knew how to use them.

FOLLOWING IN
ABSALOM'S FOOTSTEPS

Adonijah was in his late teens when he decided, "I will be king." He already looked the part: He was tall in stature, with dark eyes and dark hair and a swarthy complexion. He understood that an essential element of kingship was the ability to put on a good show—in other words, he had to act like a king. Adonijah invested in splendid chariots and magnificent horses that were guaranteed to attract attention every time he drove through the streets of Jerusalem or out into the countryside of Judah. He also hired 50 young men, all young, strong, and fleet of foot, to run before his chariot everywhere he went. This was another attention-getting device. Absalom had used it successfully, so Adonijah adopted it, too.

The fancy chariots, the pedigreed horses, the 50 runners—all this should have set off alarm bells in the royal palace, but no one said a word. Even David didn't notice. The author of 1 Kings tells us that David "had never at any time displeased him [Adonijah] by asking, 'Why have you done thus and so?'" David's obliviousness was understandable: He was a very old man by this time, spending most of his time in his private apartments trying to get warm. It's odd that in the hot climate of Judah, David always felt cold, but that was one of the trials of his old age. His servants dressed him in layer upon layer of heavy clothing, but the king still felt chilly. Finally his servants presented David with a beautiful teenage girl, Abishag, who sat in his lap or cuddled up with him in bed, and with her own body heat warmed up the king. It's a state of affairs that raises eyebrows and makes even the pure of heart a teensy bit suspicious, but the sacred author assures us, "the king knew her not." That's "know" in the biblical sense of the term.

THE FEAST ON
THE SERPENT'S STONE

New kings need allies, preferably a few from the previous regime to give the new reign a sense of continuity. Before he had himself proclaimed king, Adonijah consulted with the top men in David's court—Joab, the commander of the army of Israel; Abiathar, the only priest who had survived Saul's massacre at the sanctuary of Nob; Zadok the high priest, and Nathan the prophet; Benaiah, commander of David's bodyguard; and two of David's champions, Shimei and Rei. Out of this distinguished company, only Joab and Abiathar threw their support behind Adonijah; the rest remained loyal to David.

For what Adonijah had in mind, Joab and Abiathar weren't enough. If he was going to proclaim himself king while his father David was still alive, he needed a clean sweep with every important man of the court backing Adonijah's kingship and hustling David off to a peaceful retirement. But Adonijah's head was crammed with monarchical thoughts—there was no waiting now.

If he was going to proclaim himself king while his father David was still alive, he needed a clean sweep with every important man of the court backing Adonijah's kingship and hustling David off to a peaceful retirement. But Adonijah's head was crammed with monarchical thoughts—there was no waiting now.

At the village of Siloam, just across the Kidron Valley from Jerusalem, Abiathar and Joab proclaimed Adonijah king of Israel. To sanctify his coronation, Adonijah sacrificed an immense number of sheep and oxen. Then the new king sat down with his guests for a feast. The tables and couches had been set up on a broad plateau known as the Serpent's Stone. All of Adonijah's brothers and half-brothers had come to the coronation—all except Solomon. And all of the royal officials of Judah had shown up, too—except for Zadok, Nathan, Benaiah, and Shimei and Rei. In his euphoria, however, Adonijah didn't notice.

WHAT TO DO?

While Adonijah and his friends swilled wine, Nathan the prophet walked to the palace to call on Bathsheba. "Have you not heard," he said, "that Adonijah the son of Haggith has become king and David our lord does not know it?"

The news stunned Bathsheba. And terrified her—if Adonijah had usurped the throne, then Solomon's life was in danger, and so was hers. For that matter, so were the lives of Nathan and all the other leading men of the court who had remained loyal to David and Solomon. They were neck-deep in trouble, and could only be saved if David acted quickly. But the king was elderly and unwell; his days of riding into battle to crush his enemies were over. What were they to do?

Fortunately, Nathan had a plan. He urged Bathsheba to visit David and get him to renew his old promise that Solomon would be king. Then Nathan would join her and together they would help David crush Adonijah's rebellion.

Off Bathsheba went to her husband's rooms. The man she saw was not the impulsive, virile king who had risked everything—even his soul—to have her as his wife. This David was bent over, his hair was white, his skin was wrinkled and thin as papyrus. Young Abishag kept him wrapped in furs while she puttered about, bringing him tonics to drink. It pained Bathsheba that she must trouble her elderly, dying husband with one more worry.

Bowing to the king she delivered her news, and she didn't sugarcoat it. "Adonijah is king," she informed David, "although you, my lord king, do not know it. He has sacrificed oxen, fatlings, and sheep in abundance, and invited all the sons of the king, Abiathar the priest, and Joab the commander of the army; but Solomon your servant he has not invited. And now, my lord the king, the eyes of all Israel are upon you, to tell them who shall sit on the throne of my lord the king after him."

Then Nathan entered the room to back up everything Bathsheba had said, and impress upon David the urgency of the situation.

David sat silent for a time, pained by the betrayal of yet another son. Then, raising his right hand, he swore an oath, "As the Lord lives, who has redeemed my soul out of every adversity, as I swore to you by the Lord, the God of Israel, saying, 'Solomon your son shall reign after me, and he shall sit upon my throne in my stead;' even so will I do this day."

THE TRUE KING

To derail Adonijah's fraudulent coronation festivities, David planned a genuine one. Calling for Zadok the high priest and Benaiah commander of the royal bodyguard, David delivered his orders. "Take with you the servants of your lord, and cause Solomon my son to ride my own mule, and bring him down to Gihon; and let Zadok the priest and Nathan the prophet there anoint him king over Israel; then blow the trumpet, and say, 'Long live King Solomon!' You shall then come up after him, and he shall come and sit upon my throne; for he shall be king in my stead; I have appointed him to be ruler over Israel and over Judah."

That would take the wind out of Adonijah's sails. David was giving Solomon all the trappings of a real coronation, complete with a joint anointing by the high priest and the holiest prophet in the land, the use of the king's mule, culminating with the installation of Solomon on David's throne. Even the location for the ceremony was carefully chosen: Gihon was the site of a spring that fed the pool of Siloam. From the Serpent's Stone plateau, Adonijah and his followers would have an unobstructed view of the entire proceedings.

SOLOMON THE KING

David's men did exactly as he had instructed them. And for good measure, they brought the entire population of Jerusalem along to witness Solomon's anointing. When Zadok and Nathan had completed the ceremony, one of the guards gave a long, clear blast on the trumpet, and the people of Jerusalem cheered the new king, "rejoicing with great joy, so that the earth was split by their noise."

Meanwhile, the feast in honor of Adonijah was winding down. When the guests heard the trumpet blasts, and the music, and the other sounds of wild rejoicing, they wondered what it could be. In walked Jonathan, the son of Abiathar the priest, to explain what was going on. "King David has made Solomon king," he said. "Solomon sits upon the royal throne."

At the news Adonijah's guests scattered, running to put as much distance as they could between themselves and the usurper. As for Adonijah, he ran, too, straight to the tent where the Ark of the Covenant was kept. Trembling with fear of what Solomon might do to him, he clung to the horns of the altar; no Israelite would harm him as long he held on to the altar, but how long could he remain in this position?

GETTING OFF EASY

Solomon's victory was complete, and the lives of Bathsheba, Nathan, Zadok, Benaiah, and all the other faithful servants of David were safe. A messenger brought him the latest news regarding Adonijah. "Behold, Adonijah fears King Solomon," the messenger reported. The false king absolutely refused to let go of the sacred altar until he received a solemn promise from his half-brother: "Let King Solomon swear to me first that he will not slay his servant with the sword,"

Adonijah said. In reply Solomon sent back his own message, "If he [Adonijah] proves to be a worthy man, not one of his hairs shall fall to the earth; but if wickedness is found in him, he shall die."

The message reassured Adonijah. Relying on the tricks he had learned as a child, he released his grip on the altar and returned to the palace, where he gave every appearance of being contrite and humble. Dropping to his knees, Adonijah prostrated himself flat-out on the floor before Solomon. Solomon was a rookie king, but he knew an award-winning performance when he saw one, so he cut short the scene with his brother. All he had to say to Adonijah was, "Go to your house."

Relieved to have gotten off so easy, Adonijah went.

ADONIJAH: THE BOY WHO WOULD BE KING

WHAT ADONIJAH
can teach us

TO BE A GOOD LEADER,
BE A GOOD COMMUNICATOR

David could have spared himself and Bathsheba and Solomon and all their friends a boatload of anxiety if he had only announced his plan to make Solomon his heir. But David kept it a secret. When the Adonijah crisis came along, even Bathsheba and Nathan needed reassurance because they wondered if perhaps the old king had changed his mind.

As for Adonijah and his followers, they figured that the succession was an open question, one which they could influence. Given Adonijah's personality, he may have tried to seize the throne under any circumstances. Nonetheless, it would have been wise of David as king to state plainly who he had in mind as his successor.

"I am the good shepherd; I know my own, and my own know me."
(John 10:14)

GOD HAS A PLAN FOR YOUR LIFE

Newly graduated college students who don't find a fancy job with a big salary often feel that they've spent their whole lives preparing for a great future, only to be disappointed. Much as we sympathize with the kids, they are still young, they have so much to learn, and they will have to be patient—they aren't ready for the corner office and six-figure salary yet. As Moses and Joseph could tell us, God does not waste anyone's talents; He has a direction in mind for us all. So prepare yourself for what God has in mind for you by improving the gifts God gave you, by learning to be responsible, and by praying for wisdom to recognize the opportunity when at last it comes.

"For I would have you know, brethren, that the gospel which was preached by me is not man's gospel. For I did not receive it from man, nor was I taught it, but it came through a revelation of Jesus Christ."
(Galatians 1:11–12)

GOD WILL FORGIVE ANYONE WHO REPENTS

A ruthless king would have cut off Adonijah's head. But Solomon revealed the character of his reign (at least the early part of his reign) by showing mercy to Adonijah. In this respect he was trying to follow the example of the Lord who forgives anyone who is truly sorry. In fact, Solomon says as much when he swore to pardon Adonijah as long as his brother steered clear of any more wickedness. In the eyes of God there is no unforgivable sin, except refusing to ask for forgiveness.

"Repentance and forgiveness of sins should be preached in his name to all nations. . . . You are witnesses of these things." (Luke 24:47–48)

CHAPTER 17

REHOBOAM

THE SCORPION KING

1 Kings 11–12
2 Chronicles 11–12

Conceit. Greed. Inexperience. Injustice. Ingratitude. Rehoboam got his reign off to a wretched start, and the results were disastrous. The kingdom his father, Solomon, had built was divided, then invaded. And thanks to the silliness of old Solomon and the wickedness of young Rehoboam, a significant percentage of the people of Israel turned their backs on God to worship idols. Such a reign couldn't last forever . . .

I t's good to be king, but being a prince has its drawbacks. You spend the best years of your life waiting for Dad (or maybe Mom) to shuffle off this mortal coil so you can rule the kingdom. And history shows us that in plenty of cases the King or Queen took his or her time about going to their reward. Take Edward VI of England, son of Queen Victoria; he was almost 61 before he inherited the throne. And speaking of England, in our own day there is poor Prince Charles, nearly 60 as of this writing. His mother, Queen Elizabeth II, is 82 and still going strong. And if Elizabeth II's mother—who lived to be 101—is any indication, Prince Charles may have to wait for another two decades before he becomes king.

Like these modern English princes, Rehoboam spent his childhood, adolescence, and young manhood hanging around the palace in Jerusalem, waiting for his father Solomon to die. It sounds harsh, but that is what he was doing. Granted, he could have spent those years studying the workings of government so that when he did become king he would be a good one, maybe even a great one. Certainly he had a sound foundation on which to build: Rehoboam's father, Solomon, was the greatest king the people of Israel would ever have. Solomon was beloved by God, who appeared to him twice during his long reign. When Solomon first inherited the throne, God came to him in a dream and said, "Ask what I should give you." Solomon's answer has echoed down the ages, "Give thy servant therefore an understanding mind to govern thy people, that I may discern between good and evil." (1 Kings 3:5, 9)

Solomon's prayer for wisdom pleased God, so much so that He granted Solomon riches and honor as well, and in such generous portions that he surpassed all the other kings of the ancient world. Then the Lord made Solomon a promise. "If you will walk in my ways, keeping my statutes and commandments . . . then I will lengthen your days." (1 Kings 3:14) Was there ever an easier recipe for success? Actually, there was: God gave Adam and Eve only one "thou shalt not" commandment in Eden, and we all know how that turned out.

MR. LUCKY

Rehoboam grew up during Israel's golden age: He saw his father build the magnificent Temple for the Lord, a new palace for himself, and defensive walls around Jerusalem. The prince was a witness as Solomon erected strong cities along the borders of the kingdom to guard against any possible invasions, and he knew of the trade agreements Solomon had made with Egypt, Arabia, Tyre, and even rulers as far away as Spain and India—these trade agreements brought enormous wealth into Israel. And as if that were not enough, Solomon expanded the borders of his kingdom, too, until the realm of Israel extended from the Gulf of Aqaba in the south to the Euphrates River in the north, and the great ancient cities of Damascus and Palmyra came under Solomon's rule. The people of Israel had never known such riches, power, and prestige. And the crowning moment came when the Queen of Sheba arrived to pay homage to Solomon. In the course of her visit, she presented the king with so much gold that he couldn't find enough uses for it, so Solomon ordered his most skillful goldsmiths to fashion magnificent golden shields for 1100 officers of his army.

It was an astonishing turn of events. The Israelites began as nomads in Canaan; then they were slaves in Egypt. The Philistines had kicked them around for years until David became king and the situation improved somewhat. But the people were still, by and large, shepherds, goat herders, and farmers. Their towns and villages, even their capital, Jerusalem, were all humble, dusty, utterly forgettable places. Yet here they stood, at the pinnacle of power and prestige, a powerhouse of international trade and, most important of all, at peace with their neighbors. All of these blessings God granted to Solomon because he had kept the Lord's commandments; all of this Rehoboam would inherit. Talk about a lucky kid.

NO FOOL LIKE AN OLD FOOL

The poet Robert Frost wrote, "Nothing gold can stay." And Solomon's golden age did not even last through his lifetime.

The trouble began when the king started collecting wives and concubines from the pagan kingdoms that were either part of his realm or bordered on it. The Lord had warned the people of Israel about marrying pagan women. "You shall not enter into marriage with them . . . for surely they will turn away your heart after their gods." That is exactly what happened, even to wise old Solomon. The best families of Moab and Edom and Sidon and heaven knows what other places sent their loveliest young women to Jerusalem, and Solomon wanted them all. Before he knew it, he had 700 wives and 300 concubines, and the foolish old king "clung to these in love," as the author of 1 Kings puts it.

Flattered by the attention of so many beautiful young women, anxious that they might fall in love with the handsome young men in his court, desperately eager to keep these princesses happy, the silly old king's harem became his chief priority. From now on, Solomon's "heart was not wholly true to the Lord his God." Which is an understatement. For the sake of his foreign wives, Solomon set up pagan altars and idols of Astarte, the Phoenician fertility goddess, and of the Moabite god Chemosh, who looked like a giant fish. His wits must have become dulled by lust, because Solomon even erected a shrine to Moloch, whom the pagans worshipped by throwing their own children into a massive bonfire. These abominations angered the Lord.

Flattered by the attention of so many beautiful young women, anxious that they might fall in love with the handsome, young men in his court, desperately eager to keep these princesses happy, the silly old king's harem became his chief priority.

The people of Israel were none too happy with Solomon, either. In spite of the great wealth generated by his trade agreements, it was not enough to subsidize Solomon's opulent life style (keeping 700 wives and 300 concubines well-fed, well-housed, well-dressed, and adorned with jewels ain't cheap). And then there were the king's ambitious—and expensive—building projects. To cover these expenditures Solomon burdened his people with heavy taxes. But worse came when Solomon sent out his troops to round up strong men for forced labor at his construction sites. This was government-sanctioned slavery, and it rankled a people who had very vivid memories of their ancestors who had been slaves in Egypt.

While the people of Israel seethed with anger and resentment, Rehoboam reveled in the cushy life in his father's palace. As a teenager he daydreamed about the day when he would be king, when he would inherit great power and boundless wealth, and see the most beautiful princesses lining up to join his harem. As for the religious crisis in Israel, Rehoboam paid lip service to the Lord God, but in his heart he worshipped the pagan gods he learned about from his mother, Naamah, an Ammonite princess.

WRONG ANSWER

After 40 years on the throne of Israel, Solomon died and Rehoboam became king. Now during Solomon's reign, the land of Judah—the southern portion of the kingdom—had received the lion's share of the king's attention. It was only natural: Jerusalem, the capital, was located there; so was the little town of Bethlehem, the home of David, the birthplace of the dynasty. During all those years of David's and Solomon's reigns the ten tribes of Israel, who lived in the larger northern region of the kingdom, had felt slighted. Now they flexed their political muscles, demanding that Rehoboam should be crowned king at the holy place of Shechem in Samaria. Shechem had excellent credentials: It was the place where Abraham first settled in the Promised Land, erected an altar to the Lord, and received the promise, "To your descendants I will give this land." (Genesis 12:7) Shechem had been the home of Jacob and his large, extended family. At Shechem Joshua commanded the Israelites to disperse and take possession of the Promised Land. And it was in Shechem that the bones of Joseph, which the Israelites had carried from Egypt, were buried at last.

The place was lovely—a narrow valley only about 500 yards wide, with mountains rising all around. In this idyllic holy place a great assembly of Israelites acclaimed Rehoboam their king. Hoping to take advantage of the new king's good mood on his coronation day, a delegation approached him with a request. "Your father made our yoke heavy," the representatives of the people said. "Now therefore lighten the hard service of your father and his heavy yoke upon us, and we will serve you." But Rehoboam wasn't about to be hasty. "Depart for three days," he replied, "then come again to me."

Rehoboam hadn't chosen his council of advisors yet, so first he consulted the elderly men who had advised Solomon. Drawing upon their decades of experience, and having witnessed the trouble Solomon had brought upon the kingdom in his final years, the elderly councilors advised, "If you will be a servant to this people today and serve them, and speak good words to them when you answer them, then they will be your servants forever."

Next Rehoboam turned to his friends, the men he had known since he was a child. Basing their advice on misguided notions of entitlement and self-interest, they urged the king to say, "Whereas my father laid upon you a heavy yoke, I will add to your yoke."

Three days later, when the delegation returned to hear what Rehoboam had to say, he declared, "My father made your yoke heavy, but I will add to your yoke; my father chastised you with whips, but I will chastise you with scorpions."

SPLITSVILLE

Well, that was it, as far as the ten northern tribes of Israel were concerned. Adopting a rather poetic battle cry, they broke away from Rehoboam's kingdom and refused to acknowledge him as their king.

"What portion have we in David," they said. "We have no inheritance in the son of Jesse. To your tents, O Israel! Look now to your own house, David." In other words, the ten northern tribes of the people of Israel were renouncing their allegiance to King Rehoboam, who was a direct descendant (or of the house) of David. From now on, the northern tribes would constitute an independent kingdom.

But Rehoboam, still clueless (thanks, no doubt, to further wretched advice from his boyhood pals), did not send ambassadors to try to reunite his kingdom. Nope. He sent north a man named Adoram, who had been the taskmaster over the forced labor crews, to order the rebellious tribes to submit to Rehoboam. And Adoram had an additional message for the northern tribes: There were still all these unfinished construction projects left over from Solomon's reign—so get back to work!

The answer of the people of the northern tribes was emphatic and memorable: They stoned Adoram to death.

Now that was a reply Rehoboam understood. He hustled down to the royal stables, climbed into his fastest royal chariot, and fled from Jerusalem. But the ten tribes did not invade the southern part of the realm. Instead, they made Jeroboam their king (he had been a loyal administrator in the reign of King Solomon, and when Rehoboam came to the throne, Jeroboam had been one of the delegates sent to persuade the new king to go easy on his people).

THE BEST LAID PLANS . . .

Rehoboam's troubles were piling up—first a rebellion, now a rival king. It was obvious that the ten tribes were seceding from the union, and Rehoboam was not happy about it. He went back to Jerusalem where he called up from Judah and Benjamin—the only two tribes that were still loyal to him—180,000 troops. The army was about to march north to depose Jeroboam and bring the ten tribes back into the kingdom by force when Shemaiah the prophet walked into the camp with a message from the Lord. "You shall not go up or fight against thee your kinsmen the people of Israel. Return every man to his home, for this thing is from me." Solomon had corrupted some of his people with his cults of false gods, but there was still a large majority who had remained faithful to the God of Israel. And so, obedient to the command of the Lord delivered through His prophet, the army disbanded.

It appeared that the Lord was siding with the new northern kingdom of Israel against the southern kingdom of Judah. But then Jeroboam made an enormous mistake. He feared that if the people of the ten tribes continued to travel to Jerusalem to worship the Lord, eventually their loyalty would shift back to King Rehoboam. So he gave the people two new gods—golden calves, just like the ones their ancestors had worshipped in the Sinai desert. "You have gone up to Jerusalem long enough," Jeroboam declared to his people. "Behold your gods, O Israel, who brought you out of the land of Egypt."

Now that he felt secure on this throne, he became as bad as Jeroboam—he abandoned the worship of God to adore the idols his father had set up atop high hills. Actually, Rehoboam was worse than Solomon: He succeeded in seducing away from the Lord many people in Judah.

The priests of the Lord who had served in the northern sanctuaries refused to remain among such an unholy people; they abandoned the sanctuaries they had tended for generations and traveled to Jerusalem where they joined the staff of priests who served at Solomon's Temple. A great many Israelites, who would not become idolworshippers, also emigrated south. The Israelite émigrés strengthened Rehoboam's army; the refugee priests enhanced his moral authority; yet the king's heart was still turned against the Lord. Now that he felt secure on this throne, he became as bad as Jeroboam—he abandoned the worship of God to adore the idols his father had set up atop high hills. Actually, Rehoboam was worse than Solomon: He succeeded in seducing away from the Lord many people in Judah. These new pagans set up altars, shrines, and idols on every high hill in the country, and within the shade of every ancient tree. Furthermore, Rehoboam introduced male prostitutes in the pagan temples.

UNEXPECTED VISITORS

The male prostitutes were the last straw. The Lord, who had made Solomon wise, wealthy, and powerful, who had expanded and guarded the borders of the kingdom, now withdrew his protecting hand and permitted the king of Egypt, Shishak (we are almost 100 percent certain Shishak is Pharaoh Shoshenq I) to conquer Judah. With their 1200 chariots, 60,000 horsemen, and their vast infantry—including mercenaries from Ethiopia, Libya, and Sukkiim—the Egyptians swept across the kingdom. Rehoboam and the princes of Judah hid behind the walls of Jerusalem, hoping that Solomon's mighty defenses would save them. When the prophet Shemaiah entered the palace, the king and his attendants suspected he would not bring good news. "Thus says the Lord," Shemaiah began. "'You have abandoned me, so I have abandoned you to the hand of Shishak.'"

The thought of being massacred in the palace by the Egyptians, or dragged back in chains to be the pharaoh's slaves, brought Rehoboam and the princes to their senses. They humbled themselves before God, taking off their fine robes and putting on sackcloth, throwing ashes on their heads, and sitting barefooted on the ground where they lamented and prayed for mercy. It wasn't a show of piety; it was genuine.

The thought of being massacred in the palace
by the Egyptians, or dragged back in chains
to be the pharaoh's slaves, brought Rehoboam
and the princes to their senses.

Speaking once more to Shemaiah the prophet, the Lord said, "They have humbled themselves; I will not destroy them, but I will grant them some deliverance."

"Some deliverance." Rehoboam and the princes and the people of Judah who had turned away from God were forgiven, but they would still suffer some punishment. He permitted Shishak to conquer Jerusalem and to loot all the sacred vessels from the Temple and all the treasure from the royal palace, including those famous golden shields made in Solomon's day. But the Egyptians did not massacre the inhabitants, nor depose Rehoboam, nor lead the people of Judah back into slavery in Egypt.

As for Rehoboam, he remained faithful to God, and as a reward, after the Egyptians had left, "Conditions were good in Judah."

WHAT REHOBOAM
can teach us

BEWARE OF GREED AND BLIND AMBITION

Why do you work so hard? If it is to make a better life for yourself and your family, keep on going! If it is to exalt yourself among your neighbors—"Look at my new car! Look at the new addition I'm building onto my house!"—it is time to rethink your priorities. And not only for your own sake, but for the sake of your children. Think of the message the relentless pursuit of stuff for stuff's sake sends to the kids.

"For by the grace given to me I bid every one among you
not to think of himself more highly than he ought to think, but to
think with sober judgment, each according to the measure of faith
which God has assigned him." (Romans 12:3)

SEEK OUT SOUND ADVICE

It is easy to find people who will tell you exactly what you want to hear—whether or not what they tell you will actually do you any good. But a smart person seeks out reliable, experienced individuals who possess life wisdom. The rule of thumb is to do what is right. And sometimes—okay, more often than sometimes—that means overcoming your own selfish desires and doing the more difficult, but undeniably the right thing.

"The way of a fool is right in his own eyes; but a wise man
listens to advice." (Proverbs 12:15)

TRUE REPENTANCE EARNS GOD'S MERCY

Mercy is not a synonym for excusing bad behavior. God is merciful when we acknowledge that we have done wrong and ask for his forgiveness. No repentance, no mercy—that's the rule. The good news is that God is not satisfied to let us wallow in our sins, so he constantly calls us back. And when we respond, when we return, when we resolve by his grace to try again, then all truly is forgiven.

"Therefore the Lord waits to be gracious to you; therefore he exalts himself to show mercy to you." (Isaiah 30:18)

KEEP YOUR EYE ON THE PRIZE

The wealth, power, and prestige God bestowed upon the kingdom of Israel blinded Solomon and his son Rehoboam. Both father and son regarded these things as ends in themselves, forgetting who had granted them. The day-to-day pleasures in the palace—and there were lots of pleasures available—distracted Solomon and Rehoboam from their primary duties to God and to their people, with predictably disastrous results.

"Worthy art thou, our Lord and God, to receive glory and honor and power, for thou didst create all things, and by they will they existed and were created." (Revelation 4:11)

CHAPTER 18

AHAZIAH AND ATHALIAH

JEZEBEL'S FAMILY VALUES

1 Kings 16:29–33; 21; 2 Kings 1; 9:4–11:20

Children whose parents don't give them a good example to live by are often destined to have a hard time getting through life. Such was the case for Ahaziah and his sister, Athaliah, the privileged but unfortunate children of Jezebel and Ahab. Without guidance and with no moral grounding, the kids set out on the same dissolute path as their parents. But no people will remain subject to cruel and thoughtless rulers forever, as the wayward family would discover.

The Bonnie and Clyde of ancient Israel, Ahab the king and his queen, Jezebel, have scandalized readers of the Bible for nearly 3000 years. Ahab's name has even entered the English language, thanks to Herman Melville's epic fish story, *Moby Dick*, as a wild-eyed, obsessive maniac in open rebellion against the laws of nature and nature's God. The name Jezebel, on the other hand, has become a synonym for a willful, wicked, controlling, manipulative woman.

It should come as no surprise, then, that Ahab and Jezebel's children were horrid little brats. Ahaziah was a pint-sized glutton, and his sister Athaliah was a willful, demanding little monster who mutated into a shrieking little harpy if she did get what she wanted. These, of course, are precisely the qualities you look for in a future king and queen.

THE BACK STORY

Ahab's marriage to Jezebel, a Phoenician princess, brought a level of insane prosperity to Israel. The Phoenicians were the savviest traders in the Mediterranean at this time, and their wealth was legendary, and thanks to Jezebel's connections, Israel tapped into this commercial boom. As king, Ahab's cut was huge—so big that he built himself a palace of ivory.

In addition bringing access to easy money, Jezebel introduced to Israel her gods: Baal, the god of rain, thunder, crops, and fertility; and Astarte, the goddess of fertility and sexuality. The Israelites, going back to the days of the patriarchs, had a weakness for foreign gods. Consequently, the prophets spent a good deal of their time bringing the wayward Hebrews back to the worship of the true God.

Now it was commonplace in the kingdoms of the ancient world for a foreign queen to continue to worship the gods of her homeland when she moved to her husband's kingdom, but arrangements that were kosher in Egypt and Persia didn't apply in Israel. The law of God was very clear on the subject of worshipping false gods in the Promised Land—it was forbidden. Nonetheless, Ahab indulged his queen, erecting shrines to the Phoenician gods in Hebrew holy places, and joining her in sacrificing to Baal and Astarte. The king cheerfully permitted Jezebel to persuade Hebrews of little faith to worship these false gods; he kept silent when she declared that she was the bitter enemy of the God of Israel; and he did not raise a finger to stop his wife when she began murdering prophets of Israel by the dozens. "Ahab," the author of 1 Kings tells us, "did more to provoke the Lord, the God of Israel to anger, than all the kings of Israel who were before him." And again, "There was none who sold himself to do what was evil in the sight of the Lord like Ahab, whom Jezebel his wife incited."

AHAZIAH AND ATHALIAH: JEZEBEL'S FAMILY VALUES

A NASTY FALL

Predictably, such bad seed produced bad fruit—a son, Ahaziah, and a daughter, Athaliah. How could it be otherwise? They grew up in a household where the worship of the gods of Phoenicia was extolled and the God of Israel mocked. Their parents pursued luxury and absolute power. Their mother not only had the holy men of Israel slaughtered, but she had had a humble farmer, Naboth, arrested on a false charge of blasphemy and stoned to death. Her reason? Ahab coveted Naboth's vineyard. These were the "family values" that Ahaziah and Athaliah learned from their parents.

After Ahab was killed in battle against the Assyrians, Ahaziah succeeded him and showed everyone he was a chip off the old Ahab-and-Jezebel block. "He did evil in the sight of the Lord, and walked in the way of his father and in the way of his mother . . . He served Baal and worshipped him, and provoked the Lord, the God of Israel, to anger in every way that his father had done." Although Ahab was gone, Jezebel was still alive, and she made sure her boy Ahaziah stayed on the wrong path—adoring false gods, persecuting the faithful and the prophets of Israel.

> *Their mother not only had the holy men of Israel slaughtered, but she had had a humble farmer, Naboth, arrested on a false charge of blasphemy and stoned to death. Her reason? Ahab coveted Naboth's vineyard. These were the "family values" that Ahaziah and Athaliah learned from their parents.*

As if he did not have enough faults, Ahaziah drank to excess. After a typical bout of heavy drinking, the young king went staggering down a corridor in his palace in Samaria when he lost his footing and crashed through a latticed window. The noise of the crash, followed by the loud *thump* as Ahaziah's body struck the pavement, alerted the servants that something had gone terribly wrong. They found the king still alive but badly injured.

In a crisis it's not unusual for habitual sinners to repent, but not Ahaziah. In his sad state he did not turn to the God of his fathers, but to Baal-zebub (from whom we get the name Beelzebub), an especially foul Philistine god associated with demons and flies. Writhing on his bed, the king sent messengers to Baal-zebub's priests to hurry to the palace to heal him. But Ahaziah's messengers never got to Baal-zebub's temple—they were intercepted by the prophet Elijah, the one man in Israel who had defied Ahab and Jezebel. Warned by an angel that they were coming, Elijah met the king's messengers on the road to save them the trouble of going all the way to Baal-zebub's temple. The God of Israel had already decided Ahaziah's fate, and Elijah charged the messengers to carry the Lord's message back to the king. It was not encouraging. "Thus says the Lord," said Elijah. "'You shall not come down from the bed to which you have gone, but you shall surely die.'"

MIRACLES JUST MADE HIM MAD

Even at death's door, Ahaziah lashed out against Elijah, sending one of his captains with fifty men to arrest the prophet. They found the man of God sitting atop a hill, and when the captain called up to Elijah, demanding that he come down and surrender himself, Elijah responded by calling down fire from heaven which consumed the troop of soldiers.

Fire from heaven has been known to have a sobering effect on heathens, but this miracle only made Ahaziah mad. He sent a second captain with another fifty soldiers on the same mission, and once again Elijah reduced them to a grease spot on the road.

The third captain Ahaziah sent after Elijah had more sense and than the previous two. When he and his troop of guards arrived at Elijah's hill, the captain climbed up, knelt before the prophet and said, "O man of God, I pray you, let my life, and the life of these fifty of your servants be precious in your sight." This was the proper way to address a prophet, and Elijah was mulling over his options when an angel appeared beside him and whispered in his ear, "Go down with him, do not be afraid of him." So Elijah accompanied the third captain and his men to Ahaziah's deathbed where he delivered personally the prognosis he had sent earlier. "You shall not come down from the bed to which you have gone, but you shall surely die." Then the prophet turned on his heel and walked out of the palace. No one tried to stop him.

A short time later, Ahaziah died.

A CLEAN SWEEP

Now at that time, the Promised Land was split into two kingdoms—Israel in the north, and Judah in the south. Ahab, Jezebel, and Ahaziah ruled in Israel. Before Ahab died, he married his daughter, Athaliah, to Prince Joram, who was in line to inherit the crown of Judah. Joram and his father, King Jehoshaphat, worshipped God, but they were not so devout that they objected to Athaliah's worship of Baal and Astarte. After Jehoshaphat died, Athaliah became a kind of royal pagan missionary, just as her mother, Jezebel, had been, spreading the cult of Baal and Astarte throughout Judah, corrupting countless souls. As for her husband, the newly crowned King Joram, he did nothing to stop her. When Joram and Athaliah had a son, they named him Ahaziah, after her dissolute brother.

Athaliah's son Ahaziah was twenty-two when his father Joram died, and in the first year of his reign, the young king traveled north to Israel to visit his grandmother Jezebel and other members of his mother's family. His timing was terrible. During the young king's visit, one of the commanders of the army of the Israel, a man named Jehu, launched a palace coup against the rule of Jezebel and Ahaziah. Young Ahaziah was killed outright, and Jezebel was thrown from a window of the palace. Fearing the wrath of Jehu, no one collected the body to bury it, leaving Jezebel's corpse to be devoured by wild dogs.

But that was only the beginning. Jehu sent his men to kill the 70 sons of Ahab by his various wives and concubines. As proof that they had done their job, the soldiers cut off the princes' heads and delivered them to Jehu in baskets.

By chance, Jehu ran into 42 relatives of Athaliah who had accompanied the young King Ahaziah to Israel as his entourage. Jehu had all of them slaughtered, too. Then he marched to Samaria, where many of Ahab and Jezebel's extended family lived; before he left Samaria, Jehu and his army had wiped out the royal relatives. Finally, Jehu lured all the priests of Baal into a pagan temple, then sent in his soldiers to massacre them all.

A BLOODBATH

Athaliah could be just as bloody-minded as Jehu. When news reached her of the death of her son, Ahaziah, her mother, Jezebel, and all of her half-brothers as well as numerous cousins, aunts, and uncles, Athaliah unleashed her own massacre, sending her troops to wipe out all the descendants of King David in Judah. She did not even spare her own grandchildren.

In the pandemonium, as soldiers rampaged through the palace chasing down children, one woman, Jehosheba, made her way to the nursery where she found the prince Joash, then about one year old, cradled in the arms of his terrified nurse. Taking advantage of the chaos, the two women and the baby boy found a way out of the palace, then ran for the Temple where Jehosheba's husband, Jehoiada, served as high priest. For the next six years, while Athaliah reigned alone and unopposed over the kingdom of Judah, Joash and his nurse lived in hiding in the Temple, never once leaving it.

Jehoiada was a man who could bide his time. While Prince Joash remained out of sight (and was presumed dead by everyone in Judah and Israel), the high priest went about quietly adding to the Temple's stockpile of weapons, gathering allies in the palace and in the army, and enhancing his own standing among "the people of the land." It was all part of the priest's grand, long-term plan to depose Athaliah, overturn the pagan altars, restore the worship of the true God, and place the last legitimate descendant of King David back on the throne of his fathers.

Meanwhile Athaliah went about her business, terrorizing Judah and trying to overthrow the Lord.

A NOISY SABBATH

When Joash was seven years old, the high priest believed it was time to strike. Gathering a large band of officers and soldiers who were faithful to the Lord, he arranged to crown the little boy in the Temple. And to prove that he had the genuine article, Jehoiada brought out Joash so the commanders of the army of Judah could see that the prince was indeed alive. The high priest assigned them their places around the altar, around the Temple, and most importantly, around the boy king, saying, "The two divisions of you . . . shall surround the king, each with his weapons in his hand; and whoever approaches the ranks is to be slain." The high priest was taking a hard line, but if he planned to overthrow a queen as ruthless as Athaliah, he couldn't afford to monkey around.

On the Sabbath day the army of Judah slipped as quietly as they could into the Temple precincts where the priests armed the troops. Then all the troops hurried to their assigned places. When the worshippers arrived at the Temple that morning, they were surprised to see so many soldiers, fully armed, standing guard in the courtyards of the Temple and even around the altar. At the hour when the Temple service usually began, the high priest emerged from the Temple leading a seven-year-old boy, whom he introduced to the congregation as Prince Joash, the sole surviving heir of King David. He stood the young prince before one of the two great pillars at the front of the Temple, the traditional place where the kings of Judah were crowned. With holy oil the high priest anointed the boy, then placed a crown upon his head.

The high priest was taking a hard line, but if he planned to overthrow a queen as ruthless as Athaliah, he couldn't afford to monkey around.

At that moment the congregation's astonishment turned to joy. They leapt up, clapping their hands, and crying, "Long live the king!" The guards and the priests took up the cry, and the Temple precincts echoed with the joyful shouts.

As a confirmed heathen, Athaliah never attended services in the Temple, but when she heard the tumult, she hurried from the palace to the sanctuary. Inside she saw her grandson, Joash, wearing a crown, with the high priest Jehoiada at his side, surrounded by commanders of the army. The congregation was jubilant, and over the shouts of the people came the sound of trumpeters whose high, clear notes matched the exultation of the people of Judah.

Athaliah stood stock-still, but very quickly her shock turned to rage. In a frenzy of frustration she tore her clothes as she screamed, "Treason! Treason!" But nothing could derail the jubilation of the people in the Temple that morning. Jehoiada spotted her, however, and instructed the guards to take her outside the Temple precincts and slay her, as well as anyone who followed her. As the guards closed in around her, Athaliah bared her teeth and her nails. Shrieking, she called down the curses of her pagan gods upon the guards, the officers, the priests, and her grandson Joash. But Baal did not help her (go figure).

We have to say this much for Athaliah—after her initial outburst in the Temple, when she realized that her reign was over, she recovered her dignity, and walked back to the palace. Her troops escorted her to the courtyard in front of the stables; there they drew their swords and killed her, the last and most wicked of the children of Ahab and Jezebel.

WHAT AHAZIAH AND ATHALIAH
can teach us

KEEP THE PEACE WITHIN YOUR FAMILY

Nature has given each of us a circle of allies and supporters—it's called the family. No one will ever love you as much as your family. No one will ever work harder to help you than your family. And if you are ever truly down and out, and knock on the door of the old homestead, your family *has* to take you in. In a world full of uncertainty, the family is the one thing you can depend upon. Or it certainly should be. If your family won't give you a hand, it's time to figure out why, and resolve to fix the problem.

> *"If anyone does not provide for his own relatives, and especially*
> *for his own family, he has disowned the faith and is worse*
> *than an unbeliever." (1 Timothy 5:8)*

KEEP GOD ON YOUR SIDE

Ahab and Jezebel, Ahaziah and Athaliah—they are not alone in turning their backs on God. The dustbin of history is overflowing with characters who set themselves up to bring God down: Nero, Hitler, Stalin, Mao. Confronted with what is good, true, beautiful, and eternal, these people instead chose to ally themselves with all that is wicked, false, and cruel.

It takes a certain kind of perversity to make such a choice for evil, yet it happens every moment of every day, although rarely on the scale of the powerbrokers we just mentioned. In so many small ways, we choose daily to walk in God's path—or not. To fight against God is to take on a losing battle; to turn back to God is to win an everlasting victory.

"For we are not contending against flesh and blood, but against the principalities, against the powers, against the world rulers of this present darkness, against the spiritual hosts of wickedness in the heavenly places. Therefore take the whole armor of God that you may be able to withstand in the evil day." (Ephesians 6:12–13)

ASSERTIVENESS IS GENERALLY A GOOD THING; ABUSE OF POWER IS NOT

Athaliah had a dominant personality; she was a natural-born leader. But did she use her gifts to do good? No way. Had she not been from a royal family, she would simply have been one of those annoying, bossy people who always know what everyone else should do. But as a princess and then as queen, she learned very quickly how to force people to do what she wanted them to do. And, of course, she had the power to punish anyone who resisted her.

Power in the hands of a ruthless person is always a recipe for disaster. As we deal with others in our lives—our family, friends, coworkers, the service providers who help us out every day—it's a good idea to remember that standing up for ourselves does *not* mean manipulating others into getting our way. If running the show is giving you too big a thrill, stop and look at what's going on. Are you being fair, or heavy-handed? Ultimate authority does not exist on Earth.

"For what will it profit a man, if he gains the whole world and forfeits his life?" (Matthew 16:26)

WHEN YOU ARE CALLED UPON TO BE A LEADER, LEAD WISELY

Neither Ahaziah nor Athaliah would have come out very well in a modern-day performance review. They disrupted their kingdom, and sowed religious dissension among their people; Athaliah massacred her own family, and Ahaziah was so drunk on the job he fell out a window. The trouble was compounded when Athaliah seized control of the kingdom of Judah, although she had no right to it.

In our lives, leadership roles are usually held within our families, at work or church, or as volunteers for various organizations. Our leadership roles may not extend to a kingdom, but we still have the opportunity to make a difference for good or bad, and to affect others' lives. Fortunately, the Bible gives us many models of good leadership, such as Moses, Joshua, Deborah, and Judith. In our daily roles as parents, or in assuming leadership outside the home, it's a good idea to review stories of good leadership that inspires—and emulate the methods.

"I will seek the lost, and I will bring back the strayed,
and I will bind up the crippled, and I will strengthen the weak, and
the fat and the strong I will watch over; I will feed them in justice."
(Ezekiel 34:16)

"I am the good shepherd. The good shepherd lays down his life
for his sheep." (John 10:11)

CHAPTER 19

THE BOYS FROM BETHEL

WHO YOU CALLING "BALDY"?

2 Kings 2:23–25

Whoever coined the phrase "Sticks and stones may break my bones, but words can never hurt me," did not know the prophet Elisha. And neither did an unfortunate group of teenage boys from Bethel, who made the mistake of taunting the hair-challenged prophet, who was very sensitive to his condition, as he entered their town. For their contempt of God and his prophets, and for their inexcusable lack of decency to a stranger, the boys paid a very heavy price.

We want our children to enjoy a sense of self-confidence. We want them to be able to speak up—respectfully—in company. Certainly the last thing any parent wants is a child who is neurotically shy. But what were the parents of Bethel teaching their little boys? They saw a man, an adult and a prophet besides, approaching their town. Did they pause in the midst of their game to offer a polite greeting? Nope. They suddenly became a howling mob, dogging the heels of the visitor, mocking his physical appearance every step of the way.

It was beyond rude; it was an assault. And bear in mind, these were not adorable little tots; the Hebrew term used in 2 Kings means adolescents, boys ranging in age from 13 to 15. Even if there were only a handful sturdy enough to take on a grown man, the boys from Bethel had numbers on their side—there were at least four dozen of them, and Elisha—the prophet—was alone. The boys from Bethel were much more than a nuisance. They were a threat.

HAIR-LOSS ANXIETY

Julius Caesar was bald. Winston Churchill was bald. Yul Brynner and Telly Savalas were bald. Business leader Steve Covey is bald. So is actor Patrick Stewart, and basketball superstar Michael Jordan, and tennis champion Andre Agassi. All of them successful, admired, virile guys, perfectly at ease with their hair loss.

Alas, such was not the case with the prophet Elisha. He displayed the classic symptoms of a man who has not come to terms with his baldness: anxiety, heightened awareness of his personal appearance, hypersensitivity, anger. All these reactions, in spite of his many accomplishments.

In the first place, Elisha was the favorite disciple of the great prophet Elijah, who treated him like his own son. When Elijah was taken up to Heaven in a fiery chariot, Elisha was the only one privileged to witness the miracle. As the whirlwind carried Elijah upward, his mantle fell at the feet of Elisha—proof that by the will of the Lord, he was to be the leading prophet in Israel now.

The wonders the Lord worked through Elisha foreshadow the miracles of Jesus. He resurrected the son of the Shulamite woman. He multiplied the oil of a poor widow so she could pay off her debt to a harsh creditor and have plenty left over for her family. He healed Naaman of leprosy. He restored the fertility of the land for the farmers of Jericho. And when the children of the prophets had nothing to eat but a stew made from poisonous gourds, Elisha transformed the nasty mess into delicious, healthy food. Elisha did not make light of these tremendous graces, and no one doubts his sanctity. Still, though, he wished that he had a full head of hair.

AN INEXPERIENCED PROPHET

It was no picnic being a prophet in Israel in those days. Virtually the entire nation, led on by the king and queen, Ahab and Jezebel, had abandoned the ancient faith of Israel to worship idols of Baal and the other gods of Canaan. They had toppled the altars of God in holy places across the land, and hunted down and killed the Lord's prophets. In fear for his life, Elijah, the greatest of the prophets, fled into the mountains, but even there he kept on the move, never staying in one cave for any length of time lest Jezebel's henchmen find him.

At one point, while he was hiding in the wilderness of Beersheba, Elijah reached the end of his rope. "Now, O Lord," he prayed, "take away my life." (1 Kings 19:4) But instead of taking away his life, the Lord sent Elijah food and water through the ministry of an angel, and even revealed himself to Elijah. Strengthened and consoled, Elijah was ready to take on Ahab and Jezebel once again. It was while he was on his way back to the realm of his enemies that Elijah enlisted as his protégé Elisha, a young farmer about 25 years old, who in spite of his youth had already lost most of his hair.

After Elijah's dramatic ascension into heaven, Elisha traveled to Jericho where many sons of the prophets of Israel lived. It was there that by the power of the Lord he worked his first miracle, purifying the bitter waters. But Jericho was just a stopping point on a tour that would take Elisha north to Samaria and Mount Carmel.

His first stop was to be Bethel, a town about 20 miles from Jericho, and apparently uphill all the way: Jericho lay 1300 feet below sea level, while Bethel was 2000 feet above sea level. It was going to be a long, hot, dusty walk. And Elisha was alone, with no traveling companion to distract him from two basic facts: He was an inexperienced prophet, a rank novice, a rookie; and Bethel, firmly in the camp of Ahab and Jezebel, was a dangerous place where the Lord and his prophets were hated.

In fact, Bethel had rebelled against the Lord even before Ahab and Jezebel came to the throne. When King Jeroboam split off the ten northern tribes into the kingdom of Israel (the two southern tribes comprised the kingdom of Judah), he insisted that his people should not travel to Jerusalem to worship. He even went so far as to give the people of Israel a new, although somewhat familiar god: He set up two golden calves, one at Dan, the northernmost town in his kingdom, and the other in Bethel, his kingdom's southernmost town. Bethel, then, was a center of idol worship that recalled the golden calf the Israelites had worshipped at the foot of Sinai while Moses was up on the mountain, receiving the Ten Commandments from the hand of God.

LORD OF THE FLIES

Since Bethel was a place where God was scorned, the very least the Lord's prophets could expect was ridicule—and that's exactly what greeted Elisha, as weary, hot, thirsty, and irritable, he drew near the gates of the town. Suddenly, as if out of nowhere, a crowd of about four dozen young teen boys came running up to the prophet, jeering, "Go up, you baldhead!" In modern parlance we would translate this as, "Get outta here, baldy!"

Bethel, like all the towns and villages of Israel and Judah, was a dull place where excitement and visitors were both rare. For the hellions of Bethel, who were brimming over with adolescent energy, and with no suitable outlet for it, the arrival of Elisha was a golden opportunity: He was a stranger, a young man prematurely bald, and a despised prophet of the hated of God of Israel besides. Never before had they had so much material to work with.

Running along side Elisha, they continued their jeering, heaping contempt on the stranger who was wearing the mantle of Elijah, the prophet their parents and every other adult in Bethel remembered

THE BOYS FROM BETHEL: WHO YOU CALLING "BALDY"?

with loathing. With so many adolescent boys all focused on one object of derision, it wouldn't have taken much for rude words to make the transition to violent deeds. One rock thrown by one especially bold kid and Elisha would have found himself in the middle of a pack of armed and dangerous teenagers; another minute, and it would have become a scene out of *Lord of the Flies*.

Now, as cutting remarks go, "Go up, you baldhead" is fairly tame. A witty man could have disarmed the boys with a joke at his own expense. A more self-confident man would have ignored the little rascals, or perhaps picked up a stout stick from the road and scared them off. But this mockery of his hairless head made Elisha a mite peevish. He called down the wrath of the Lord on the unruly teens. The curse in the name of the God of Israel provoked the boys to a fresh round of abuse, profanity, and scorn. So intent were they on Elisha that none of them heard the heavy tread and snuffling sound of the two she-bears who lumbered out of the woods and approached the boys from the rear. Suddenly there was a terrible roar, followed by more terrible screams of pain and panic as the bears tore into the crowd of boys. Young and nimble though they were, they couldn't escape the animals; the bears pursued them, growling, lashing out with their razor-sharp claws, tearing the boys of Bethel to pieces. When the bears stopped at last, it was deathly still outside Bethel and the bodies of forty-two boys lay scattered across the countryside.

One rock thrown by one especially bold kid and Elisha would have found himself in the middle of a pack of armed and dangerous teenagers; another minute, and it would have become a scene out of Lord of the Flies.

The stories the Old Testament tells about Elisha portray him as a man full of mercy and pity who called upon the Lord to work miracles for the sake of helpless people, including children. What turned him against the boys from Bethel? Because they and their parents were already cursed by God, as the Lord had warned the Israelites when he gave them the law in the wilderness: "Then if you walk contrary to me, and will not hearken to me . . . I will let loose the wild beasts among you, which shall rob you of your children, and destroy your cattle, and make you few in number, so that your ways shall become desolate." (Leviticus 26:21–22)

It was a tough lesson, but the people of Israel had been warned.

As for Elisha, the massacre did not trouble him in the least, and so he continued on to Mount Carmel, and then to Samaria. He felt pleased and grateful that the Lord had avenged him. His dignity had been upheld, and once the story got around, it was a safe bet that no other mob of rude kids would call him names.

WHAT THE BOYS FROM BETHEL
can teach us

ENOUGH IS ENOUGH

The people of the Old Testament would not have used the phrase "tough love," but they would have understood the concept. Children, especially rebellious, self-destructive teens, can cause serious harm to themselves and to their families unless parents are willing to stand their ground and state as clearly as possible that there are certain kinds of behavior the family will not tolerate. It was not just the boys outside the town gates who had gotten out of hand, the entire population of Bethel was in open rebellion against God. The mockery and threats against Elisha roused God's anger, and he so he taught the people of Bethel a lesson they would never forget. For that matter, no one else has forgotten it either!

"You shall know that I am in the midst of Israel, and that I, the Lord, am your God and there is none else." (Joel 2:27)

RESPECT THE CLERGY

The clergy dedicate their lives to the service of the Lord and the service of the Lord's people. For this reason they deserve to be treated respectfully. Of course, their ministry doesn't make them perfect, and there will always be some members of the clergy—fortunately, only a very few—who will disgrace themselves and scandalize the community of believers. To mistreat a member of the clergy is an insult to the Lord who sent this person to minister to the church.

"Now I rejoice in my sufferings for your sake, and in my flesh I complete what is lacking in Christ's afflictions for the sake of his body, that is, the church, of which I became a minister according to the

divine office which was given to me for you, to make the word of God
fully known, the mystery hidden for ages and generations, but now
made manifest to his saints." (Colossians 1:24–26)

BE KIND

Love God, love your neighbor. They are two essential parts of the
same commandment. Since God is the Creator and Father of us all,
we are all brothers and sisters. The boys of Bethel didn't see Elisha—
a stranger who never had done them any harm—as a brother because
they did not acknowledge God as their Father.

How then should we treat strangers? With courtesy first of all,
with kindness, and with generosity as far as our means and condition
of life will allow.

"Come, O blessed of my Father, inherit the kingdom prepared for you
from the foundation of the world; for I was hungry and you gave me
food, I was thirsty and you gave me drink, I was a stranger and you
welcomed me." (Matthew 25:34–35)

DON'T MAKE FUN OF THE WAY
PEOPLE LOOK

Even today, there is only so much a gym membership, cosmetic
surgery, and hair plugs can do to alter the way we look. To become
obsessed about the imperfections in your own physical appearance is
vanity; to openly ridicule the physical imperfections of other people
is cruelty. If you see your kids teasing someone, don't tolerate the
behavior—the odds are good the kids won't indulge in such mean-
ness when they grow up, if you nip it in the bud early. Beauty fades,
muscles sag, hair falls out, but a good heart is forever young and
pleasing to the Lord.

"The crucible is for silver and the furnace is for gold, and the Lord
tries the heart." (Proverbs 17:2) "Let the words of my mouth and medi-
tation of my heart be acceptable in thy sight, O Lord, my rock and my
redeemer." (Psalm 19:14)

CHAPTER 20

MANASSEH

THE LITTLE PRINCE

2 Kings 21:1–18
2 Chronicles 33:1–20

Manasseh was the rotten kid who never grew up. At 12, when Manasseh became king upon his father's death, his self-centered rages were even more disturbing: Now, he was a rotten kid with unchecked power. He always insisted upon having his own way, no matter how wrong or how many people he hurt—and he hurt a lot of people. Could such a totally unregenerate human being ever truly repent and be forgiven?

Hollywood has made millions turning out movies that feature sinister children. Think of Damian in *The Omen*, or the coven of devilish farm kids in *The Children of the Corn*. Evil children are much more frightening than any adult psychopath in a goalie mask running amok at an isolated summer camp, because children are innocent of true evil. They're naughty, they're rambunctious, they're selfish, and sometimes they lash out, hitting, kicking, or biting whoever has gotten between them and the desired object. But a time-out or a dinner without dessert usually checks such bad behavior.

If Queen Hepzibah had ever tried to give her son Manasseh a time-out, the little tyke probably would have laced her morning coffee with strychnine. Manasseh is one of those scary kids of the horror movies come to life, and his wickedness is chilling, not to mention precocious. Every seventh or eighth grade classroom has at least one willful, contrary kid whose main joy in life is shocking the adults. But in Manasseh's case it was different: He was a rotten kid who delighted in doing bad stuff, and as king he had the power to accomplish whatever he wished, no matter how dreadful. So, one by one, the boy-king smashed the taboos of the faith of Israel.

FROM WORSE TO WORSER

It breaks the heart to think of it, but time after time, in spite of all the signs and wonders the Lord wrought out of love for his chosen people, the Israelites turned away from the true God to worship the idols of their neighbors. The Canaanite gods, Baal and Astarte, were especially popular, no doubt because their worship involved visits to temple prostitutes as well as participation in fertility cults (a fancy academic phrase that means "orgies").

When Hezekiah became king of Judah, he tore down the shrines and temples of the pagan gods, smashed the idols, and then set a good example for his people by worshipping God alone. "He held fast to the Lord," the author of 2 Kings tells us, "he did not depart from following him, but kept the commandments which the Lord commanded Moses. And the Lord was with him; wherever he went forth, he prospered." As a further reward for Hezekiah's faithfulness, when Sennacherib, king of Assyria, laid siege to Jerusalem—a siege which Hezekiah had no chance of breaking—the Lord sent an angel into the Assyrian camp to slay 185,000 of the enemies of Judah. The next morning, when Sennacherib awoke to find himself surrounded by an army of corpses, it occurred to him that this would be a good time to break camp and head for home.

How such a good king, for whose sake the Lord was willing to work a miracle, could have produced such a nasty child as Manasseh is a mystery. By the time Manasseh was 12—his age when his father,

Hezekiah, died and little Manasseh became king of Judah—he was already a mean, spiteful child. Immediately the boy-king set about overturning all the good work his father, King Hezekiah, had accomplished. He raised up on hilltops altars to the Canaanite gods, Baal and Astarte. He made a public show of his worship of the entire Canaanite pantheon, encouraging all the people of Judah to follow his bad example. In an act of brazen sacrilege, Manasseh even installed an altar bearing an idol of the Canaanite fertility goddess, Astarte, inside the holy Temple in Jerusalem. He erected yet more heathen altars in the Temple's two courtyards, and since he wanted his temple to be as authentic as any in Canaan, he introduced "sacred" prostitutes into the Temple precincts.

And it only got worse. Manasseh brought in mediums to contact the spirits of the dead; he consulted soothsayers to learn the future; he commanded wizards to cast spells against his enemies. And then Manasseh outdid himself. After he married (can you imagine what his wife must have been like?) he offered his own son, a little child, as a human sacrifice, burning the little boy alive on the altar of the god Moloch. The terrible place where this terrible crime took place is called a tophet, and it was located in the Valley of Hinnom, southwest of Jerusalem. In Hebrew, the Valley of Hinnom is "Ge Hinnom," or "Gehenna." Years later, after Manasseh was dead and the altar of Moloch had been razed to the ground, the memory of the awful things that took place there still haunted the people of Judah, and they began to use the name Gehenna as the Hebrew term for Hell.

INIQUITY LOVES COMPANY

Most sinners try to hide the evil they do, but Manasseh sinned flagrantly and in the eyes of the world. Most sinners have some shred of conscience that makes them feel guilty, nudging them towards repentance, but Manasseh reveled in his sins. Iniquity loves company, and

Manasseh convinced many of the people of Judah to join him in this orgy of sin. He "seduced them to do more evil than the nations had done whom the Lord destroyed before the people of Israel."

This is another facet of hardcore wickedness—self-destructive behavior. Time and again throughout their turbulent history, the Israelites had witnessed what happened to people who mocked God. The flood had scoured the earth clean of an unholy people. Fire from heaven had consumed the wicked cities of Sodom and Gomorrah. The earth had opened and swallowed up Dathan, Korah, and Abiram. Did Manasseh and his followers really think they would escape unscathed?

The answer is, "Yes!" Their perverted hearts had persuaded them that only the gods of the Canaanites were real, that the God of Israel either did not exist, or that he was powerless to harm them. Manasseh and his followers were asking for it. And, as if God needed any more provocation, they began to murder citizens of Jerusalem who remained faithful to the Lord, refusing to take part in the heathen sacrifices and obscene rites of Baal, Astarte, and Moloch. The king "shed very much innocent blood, till he had filled Jerusalem from one end to the other." According to an ancient Jewish tradition, which many of the early Christians also believed, it was during this time that the great prophet Isaiah died a martyr: Manasseh, the story goes, ordered Isaiah to be sawn in two.

"I will wipe Jerusalem as one wipes a dish," the Lord promised his heartsick prophets, "wiping it and turning it upside down."

MORE THAN HE DESERVED

Manasseh's punishment was dreadful. The Lord unleashed on Israel the Assyrians, the Nazis of the ancient world, an absolutely merciless people who could be very inventive when it came to cruelty. The Assyrians attacked Jerusalem, and this time no angel came down from heaven to stop them. They swarmed over the walls, slaughtering the Judean soldiers on the battlements and the civilians they found in the streets. They smashed down the gates of the royal palace, massacred Manasseh's guard, then searched through every room until they found the king, whom they took alive.

The Assyrians bound Manasseh with bronze chains, then pierced his jaw with hooks. By the tether attached to the hooks, they led the king, who was in agony, through the streets of his conquered capital city. As the procession made its way through the city, Assyrian troops paused in their killing and pillaging to cheer the terrible sight. In this awful condition, Manasseh was dragged by the Assyrian commander all the way to Babylon, where the chains were struck off his wrists and ankles, and the hooks removed from his jaws before he was locked in a foul prison cell.

In great pain, and filled with terror at what the Assyrians might do to him next, Manasseh "entreated the favor of the Lord his God and humbled himself greatly before the God of his fathers." God heard the king. If He sent him spiritual consolation, that would have been more than enough, and certainly more than Manasseh deserved. But the king's repentance was so heartfelt that the Lord treated Manasseh with great mercy. He healed the king of his terrible wounds, and He moved the Assyrians to release Manasseh and send him back to Jerusalem. "Then," the author of 2 Chronicles tells us, "Manasseh knew the Lord was God."

Back in his capital, Manasseh got busy. "He took away the foreign gods and the idols from the house of the Lord, and all the altars that he had built on the mountain of the house of the Lord and in Jerusalem, and he threw them outside the city. He also restored the altar of the Lord, and offered upon it sacrifices of peace offerings and of thanksgiving; and he commanded Judah to serve the Lord the God of Israel."

For the rest of his life, Manasseh remained steadfast in his worship of the true God. It was as thorough a conversion as anyone could hope for and, given Manasseh's history, entirely unexpected.

WHAT MANASSEH
can teach us

BE FOREWARNED: KIDS WILL ALWAYS WANT TO RUN THE SHOW

When Mommy or Daddy won't let a toddler have what he or she wants—attention, a cookie, a new toy—it's not unusual for the little darling to unleash an ear-splitting temper tantrum. But frustration is only one source of tantrums; the perfectly natural desire to be in charge, to act independently, to take control of a situation, all of these things may be running through the kid's head, and if these requirements aren't being met, then it's melt-down time. But indulging the kid will only send him or her the message, "This is how I can get what I want." The early years of Manasseh's reign were one long tantrum, but because it slipped the minds of the people around him that he was a child first and a king second, they found themselves living in a hissy fit that swiftly developed into a national nightmare.

"When you walk, they [your parents] will lead you; when you lie down,
they will watch over you; and when you wake, they will talk with you.
For the commandment is a lamp and the teachings a light."
(Proverbs 6:22–23)

KINGS AND PARENTS HAVE A LOT IN COMMON

In olden days political commentators often portrayed a king as the father of a national family, or the shepherd of a national flock. But whether the job is as king, shepherd, or parent, the essential qualifications of the job—care, affection, watchfulness, and a recognition of the necessity of setting limits—are the same. Manasseh did not just tyrannize his people, he encouraged them to turn away from what was good and do evil. Worse, he killed anyone who had the gumption to resist his will (apparently Manasseh never outgrew those temper tantrums).

"For it is God's will that by doing right you should put to silence the ignorance of foolish men. Live as free men, yet without using your freedom as a pretext for evil; but live as servants of God."
(1 Peter 2:15–16)

NO ONE, HOWEVER BAD, IS BEYOND HOPE

God's grace is a mystery. It can penetrate even the most hardened heart. In fact, every moment of every day, it stands there knocking on the door of the stone-cold heart, waiting for the moment when the poor goof of a sinner finally lets grace in. But that's the tough part: Sin turns us away from everything that is good, and true, and holy, and the longer we remain stewing in our own badness, the less likely we are to repent. But the prayers of family and friends can help. Certainly someone must have been praying for Manasseh.

"Wash yourselves; make yourselves clean; remove the evil of your doings from before my eyes; cease to do evil, learn to do good; seek justice, correct oppression; defend the fatherless, plead for the widow." (Isaiah 1:16–17)

YOU DON'T HAVE TO WAIT UNTIL THINGS ARE AT THEIR WORST TO REPENT

The Good Thief didn't regret his life of crime until he was hanging on his cross. The Prodigal Son did not regret his life of dissipation until he was so starved that pig slop looked mighty appetizing. And when did Manasseh come to his senses? After his kingdom had been conquered, his face had been mutilated, and he had been dragged in chains to a dungeon in a far-off land. The cross, the starvation, and the prison cell all got the attention of these sinners, and that tends to be the story (although in a less dramatic form) for all of us. It's when we hit rock bottom and think of how thoroughly we've messed up our lives that we turn to God. He will welcome us back, of course, but He would have taken us back sooner, if we'd only had the sense to repent before things got really bad.

"Restore us to thyself, O Lord, that we may be restored!
Renew our days as of old!" (Lamentations 5:21)

CHAPTER 21

SALOME

ALL THE RIGHT MOVES

Mark 6:21–29
Matthew 14:6–11

With guidance and limitations set by caring parents, Salome might have been just another girl, doing her best to get through puberty. But that was not Salome's fate. Sexually precocious, and with a wanton father and vindictive mother—neither of whom seemed capable of giving a child genuine love and guidance—Salome always got what she asked for. One day, what Salome asked for was simply too horrible, an act that flouted the laws of God and of man.

She was the Lolita of Jerusalem, a not-quite-legal temptress sprung from a family that made a habit of incest. She is one of the vilest children in Sacred Scripture, yet the two gospels that tell her story, Mark and Matthew, fail to tell us her name, as if the evangelists wanted the little vixen's identity to be lost forever. If it weren't for the first century A.D. Jewish historian Josephus, we would never have learned that the name of the teenage vamp who asked for the head of John the Baptist on a plate was Salome.

Salome was one of those teenage girls who knew she was hot, and figured out how to use her looks to get what she wanted. She had no interest in manipulating boys her age—that would have been too easy. Aside from being pimply and overeager, teenage boys could not offer her the things she really wanted—power, or better yet domination, especially over mature men. To get a man who should have known better to do her will was thrilling, and Salome never tired of experiencing that thrill.

FAMILY TIES

Sorting out the connections in this family is complicated, so hang on. Salome's mother was Herodias; Salome's father was Herod II. Herod II was also Herodias' uncle. After a little more than twenty years of marriage (during which time Salome was born), Herodias divorced Herod II and married another of her uncles, Herod Antipas. As a young woman, Salome continued the family tradition by marrying one of *her* uncles, her mother's brother Philip.

Marrying within the family created a very tangled web of relationships for all the family members. As for Salome, she was:

- Both the grandniece and the daughter of her father, Herod II;
- Both the niece and the wife of her husband, Philip;
- Both the daughter and the sister-in-law of her mother, Herodias.

No wonder John the Baptist targeted this insanely in-bred clan. His repeated public denunciations of the marriage of Herod Antipas and Herodias enraged the queen. How dare a shaggy, sunburned wild man of the desert condemn her? Every time John preached against her, Herodias threw a very unregal tantrum, demanding that the king arrest and execute the plain-talking prophet, who spoke only the truth.

After months of unremitting goading and nagging, Herod Antipas at last gave in to his wife and ordered his soldiers to find John and throw him into prison. But the king refused to sentence John to death. Perhaps there was some part of Herod Antipas' heart that could still feel pangs of guilt over unjustly imprisoning an innocent man. Perhaps there was some small corner of his conscience that still believed "Fear of the Lord is the beginning of wisdom." And let's not rule out the possibility that the king may have had a superstitious dread of what might happen to him if he killed a holy man. Whatever his reasons, Herod left John in prison, but did not harm him.

STRIKE UP THE BAND

The formula for a successful birthday party has not changed over the last 2000 years: guests, food, entertainment, and lots of presents. As king, Herod could bump up the festivities a few notches, but aside from fancy eats and gold tableware, the birthday party Herod threw for himself was pretty much like any other.

In honor of his special day, Herod invited all the prominent men of Galilee, all the officers of his guard, and all the commanders of his army to join him for a banquet at the palace. All night long, the palace slaves served course after course of delectable food to the king and his guests, and kept their cups filled to overflowing with wine. By the end of the meal Herod was drunk, but he wasn't ready to go sleep it off yet. He wanted to see the entertainment, so he called upon Salome to dance for him.

Young, lithe, lovely, and blessed with a great sense of rhythm, Salome could have made a career as a professional dancer, but in those days it was considered bad form for a princess to go on the stage. So when Salome danced, it was only for family and friends. Herod, of course, had seen Salome dance many times, and even when he wasn't intoxicated he found her moves intoxicating. His speech slightly slurred by the wine, the king begged Salome to dance for him.

Young, lithe, lovely, and blessed with a great sense of rhythm, Salome could have made a career as a professional dancer, but in those days it was considered bad form for a princess to go on the stage.

The girl was savvy beyond her years, but she was still a girl: she glanced at her mother for approval; Herodias nodded, and Salome left her place at the table to take center stage before the king and his guests. The musicians began to play, and Salome began to dance. She had no inhibitions, no self-restraint; she flaunted her youth, her beauty, and as much of her body as she dared. Some of the guests lowered their eyes—she was, after all, so young, it was not proper to ogle the girl. But many others were captivated by Salome's performance. They had never seen anything so alluring.

"WHAT SHALL I ASK?"

By the time the music stopped and the dance was over, drunken Herod was inflamed with passion. Eager to gratify the girl so she would gratify him later, the king declared, "Ask me for whatever you wish, and I will grant it." Salome, who had learned from her mother the art of making a man wait, gave the king no answer. So Herod Antipas sweetened the offer. "Whatever you ask me, I will give you, even half of my kingdom." Half a kingdom in exchange for the favors of a teenage girl. The king was humiliating himself in front of his guests, but at this moment he was insensible to shame.

Still, Salome did not answer. She ran to her mother, who was reclining on a couch, and whispered to her, "What shall I ask?" Herodias, she-wolf that she was, gave no thought to what might benefit her daughter for the rest of her life—the gold, jewels, or half a kingdom that the rash, drunken Herod had just sworn to hand over at Salome's request. Instead, Herodias' mind was filled with thoughts of revenge.

"What shall I ask?" Salome repeated, breathlessly anticipating her mother's answer. Herodias' lips curled into a sly smile. She turned to Salome, looking her straight in the eyes. In a firm and controlled voice, she replied, "The head of John the Baptist."

A thrilling, sadistic sensation ran through Salome. She smiled to herself, then turned and hurried back to the king. Standing before Herod Antipas and all his guests, in a loud, clear voice Salome declared, "I want you to give me at once the head of John the Baptist on a platter." The part about the head "on a platter" was Salome's inspiration. Herodias was so proud. What mother wouldn't be?

In spite of his impaired condition, Herod was horrified; he could barely believe he had heard Salome's request correctly. But looking into her malevolent eyes, he knew that he had. Howling with grief and rage, Herod buried his face in his hands. There was nothing he could do; he had sworn an oath to the girl in front every distinguished man in Galilee. He had no choice but to keep his word. He beckoned one of his guards and gave him orders to take John from his cell, cut off his head, place it on a dish, and bring John's severed head to the banquet hall.

What must the atmosphere have been like in that room in the palace, while everyone waited for the guard to carry out his orders? In such festive surroundings, on such a happy occasion, did Herod ever have any insight into the horror he had a hand in creating? Did guests sob in disbelief? Did anyone dare to utter a word of regret?

A little while later, the guard returned with the grisly trophy. He carried it first to Herod Antipas, but the king recoiled in horror; he would not even look at it. Stifling a sob, he waved in the direction of Salome. And so the guard carried the platter to Salome, who reached across the table to receive it, smiling as she took it from the hands of the guard. Then rising carefully so as not to drop it, Salome presented the platter with the severed head to her mother. Together, mother and daughter left the banquet hall with their prize.

WHAT CAN SALOME
teach us?

HEAVY DRINKING MIXED WITH HEAVY PARTYING IS A RECIPE FOR TROUBLE

Given everything else that happens in this story, the fact that Herod Antipas had a few too many at his own party seems like a minor point. Yet it was because he was drunk that he lost control of himself. His lechery went into high gear, and, blinded by desire for Salome, he promised to give her anything she wanted. He became a man out of control—and it began with heavy drinking.

Under the influence of too much alcohol, we are all capable of shameful acts and empty promises. Fortunately, most of us are also capable of monitoring how much we drink. It's a good idea to set limits.

"Let us then cast off the works of darkness and put on the armor of light; let us conduct ourselves becomingly as in the day, not in reveling and drunkenness, not in debauchery and licentiousness, not in quarreling and jealousy. But put on the Lord Jesus Christ, and make no provision for the flesh, to gratify its desires." (Romans 13:12–14)

POWER, ABSOLUTE AND UNCHECKED, IS NEVER A GOOD THING TO HAVE OR TO BESTOW ON ANOTHER

Time and again, the Bible reminds us that legitimate authority comes from God, and that anyone who abuses his or her authority will have to answer to Him. But in their pursuit of power, Herodias and Salome did not give God a thought. The mother waited for the moment when she could kill John the Baptist, while the daughter savored her ability to captivate a king. Because the idea of self-restraint apparently never occurred to Herodias and Salome, and because no one had dared impose limits on their power, the two carried out one of the most dastardly crimes in the literature of the Bible.

"He has shown strength with his arm, he has scattered the proud in the imagination of their hearts." (Luke 1:51)

SOMETIMES, THE WICKED DO SEEM TO HAVE THE UPPER HAND

Christ Himself said, "Truly I say to you, among those born of women there has risen no one greater than John the Baptist." (Matthew 11:11) Yet even John, holy, innocent, and great as he was, fell victim to a wicked mother-and-daughter team.

In our own lives, we often experience what seems to us to be evil—although not on so dramatic a scale as this. Evil might come in the form of spiteful neighbors or malicious coworkers, in the tragic death of a loved one or the terminal illness of a child, in serious financial troubles and deals gone wrong. When it appears that the bad guys have the upper hand, remember that their success is for the short-term only. As you struggle to regain your footing and stand tall, remind yourself that in the struggle of bad vs. good, an earthly victory is not the ultimate victory.

"Though a sinner does evil a hundred times and prolongs his life, yet I know that it will be well with those who fear God . . . but it will not be well with the wicked." (Ecclesiastes 8:12–13)

ALWAYS BE AWARE OF THE LESSONS YOU ARE TEACHING YOUR CHILDREN

First question: Who taught Salome how to dance? Second question: When she saw *how* her daughter danced, why didn't Herodias cancel all future dance lessons? Did Herodias turn a blind eye as Salome grew up to be a sexually precocious adolescent? More likely she trained Salome to be so—Salome's overt sexuality would be just one more tool she could use to manipulate Herod Antipas. How disturbing is that?

Most parents, of course, would never stoop to Herodias' level. Even so, it's wise to remember that your children are always looking to you as an example. You are sending them into the world with the lessons your words and actions teach them, every day.

"Hear O Israel: The Lord our God is one Lord; and you shall love the Lord our God with all your heart, and with all your soul, and with all your might. And these words which I command you this day shall be upon your heart; and you shall teach them diligently to your children." (Deuteronomy 6:4–7)

CHAPTER 22

THE PRODIGAL SON

THE PARTY'S OVER

Luke 15:11–32

As a lad, the Prodigal Son was charming and fun to be around, the life of every party. Unfortunately, he grew into a wayward and thoughtless young man, turning his back on his doting father and responsible brother and squandering his inheritance for the sake of having a good time. Then one day, the money ran out . . . where was the Prodigal Son to go?

Y ou just know that as a kid, the Prodigal Son was the family cutup, the bold, precocious little boy whose outrageous comments could make a roomful of adults roar with laughter. He liked the attention, and he learned that if he was careful, if he teased but never insulted the grownups, he would be everybody's favorite. It was also a nifty way to steal the limelight from his big brother—the solid, dependable kid who could always be counted on to do his homework and turn in his school projects on time.

In his teen years, when his indulgent father was giving him a generous allowance, the Prodigal Son began cultivating his own friends. He still liked to be the center of attention, and he found that if he picked up the check at the end of an evening out with his friends, all the cool guys would want to hang out with him and all the prettiest girls would want to date him.

It got to the point where the Prodigal Son's craving for attention and adulation extended to complete strangers. Once again, he found that money was the key: All he had to do was buy a few rounds of drinks, and everyone in the tavern was his best friend. Things could get even friendlier if he gave some pricey bauble to a girl who was fun to party with, but not the type he could bring home to meet Dad. Tragically (from his point of view), the Prodigal Son did not have an unlimited income, a situation he found galling because he usually blew through his allowance in the first ten days of the month.

He began to daydream about the death of his father, when he would receive his share of the family estate. At first the Prodigal Son was ashamed of such thoughts, but soon he became accustomed to them. After all, he was only contemplating the inevitable; he wasn't plotting to bump off the old man. Then, one day, he thought of a way out of his predicament. He sought out his father and said, "Father, give me the share of property that falls to me."

That was a painful moment for the good old man. He knew that his son squandered money; he knew if he gave his boy his share of his inheritance now, he would run through it in no time. The kid simply could not be trusted with cash. But this father's love for his son was so great that he did as the boy asked, and had his steward hand over to the Prodigal Son fat bags of gold coins. The oldest son was livid but he kept his mouth shut, went on with his work, and hoped his snotty kid brother would take the gold and go—he never thought his little brother had been of any use anyway.

He began to daydream about the death of his father, when he would receive his share of the family estate. At first the Prodigal Son was ashamed of such thoughts, but soon he became accustomed to them. After all, he was only contemplating the inevitable; he wasn't plotting to bump off the old man.

LIVING THE HIGH LIFE

After a few days, the Prodigal Son did pack up his belongings. Weighed down with his bags of gold, he traveled first class to a far-off, pagan country. There he found that no matter where you are, people are just the same. Buy the drinks, buy the dinner, give the ladies a few gifts, and the locals just couldn't be friendlier. At last he had what he had always wanted—no responsibilities, no disapproving parent, no budget, and a world where he was always the center of attention. And so he partied on.

One morning, he woke up with a killer hangover, as usual. He thought he would feel better if he went out for some breakfast, so he staggered over to the chest where he kept his inheritance. He looked inside. All he saw was empty bags. He began to paw through the chest—surely there was a bag of gold at the bottom of the chest—but he just found more empty bags. The Prodigal Son panicked, tossing bags over his shoulders and dumping the chest out on the floor as he searched frantically. But there was no more gold, not a single coin. He had squandered it all. The Prodigal Son flopped down on the bed and tried to think: He was hungry, he was hung-over, and he was broke. What was he going to do now?

The answer was obvious—he would go to his friends! He had always been good to them; just the night before, they had said how much they loved him. His friends would take care of him.

At the first house he visited, the Prodigal Son was welcomed with open arms, but when he explained his dire situation, his friend's mood turned very serious. There was a famine in the land, his friend said, and he had to keep an eye on his provisions so he wouldn't run out. Taking in a long-term houseguest at such a time was impossible.

Surprised and stung by the rejection, the Prodigal Son went to the home of another of his friends, where he was met with the same sad excuses. Times were so uncertain, it wouldn't be prudent to take in a houseguest.

The Prodigal Son could not admit to himself that his "friends" had never really cared about him and had only been using him. In his denial, he would not acknowledge what he knew deep inside to be true—that his father's house was the one place where he would be welcomed and cared for and given second, third, and fourth chances, right up to seventy times seven chances to straighten himself out. His father had always loved him, and always would, no matter what.

But the Prodigal Son was obstinate. He would not return to his father and admit the error of his ways.

REALITY CHECK

Meanwhile, word was spreading throughout the city that the Prodigal Son was broke and looking for someone to take him in. The man who had once been hailed as the life of every party was now spurned as a freeloader, a deadbeat. By the end of the day, servants were turning him away at the door: The master was not at home; the master was indisposed; the master could not see any more petitioners that day.

The Prodigal Son had failed utterly to find a single friend willing to help him, but he had heard about a man who needed farm workers. And so the Prodigal Son went to see the man, applied for a job, and was hired on the spot, sent out to the fields to feed his employer's swine. The boy had known that he was living in a pagan country, of course, but it came as a shock that he, a son of Israel, could only keep himself alive if he tended the animals he had been brought up to regard as the most unclean. That belief certainly seemed true to him: Even from a long way off, the stench of the pig farm was so bad that he couldn't help gagging.

Every day, servants from the city brought to the farm fodder for the swine and food for the Prodigal Son. The pigs ate castoffs from the master's kitchen, and lots of them; the Prodigal Son received a few scraps. He was tempted to keep some of the pigs' food for himself, a thought which made him gag all over again. "How many of my father's servants have bread enough, and to spare," he said to himself, "but I perish here with hunger!" It was the first rational thought the boy had had in years. And now that his mind was engaged, he understood what he must do—repent!

"I will arise and go to my father, and I will say to him, 'Father, I have sinned against heaven and before you; I am no longer worthy to be called your son; treat me as one of your hired servants.'" Before he gave himself to chance to change his mind, the Prodigal Son abandoned the pigs and started walking home.

HOME AGAIN

It was a terrible journey. He was hungry when he started out, and he had to beg for food all along the way. On most days he was on the verge of starvation; he slept outdoors in all weather; he didn't have proper footwear for such a hike, so his feet became two big blisters. Who knew that repentance would be so painful?

At last he could see his father's house far in the distance; he was truly in the home stretch now. Then he noticed a small group of people running toward him, with one man clearly leaving all the other runners in the dust. It was his father! Weeping, the old man embraced his boy and kissed him. The Prodigal Son was stunned, but he began to say the speech he had rehearsed over and over along the road. "Father, I have sinned against heaven and before you," he said. "I am no longer worthy to be called your son."

Before he could finish, his father called to the servants who had followed him. "Bring quickly the best robe, and put it on him; and put a ring on his hand, and shoes on his feet; and bring the fatted calf and kill it, and let us eat and make merry; for this my son was dead and is alive again; he was lost, and is found."

The Prodigal Son could scarcely believe what he was hearing. No reproaches, no recriminations, no cries of "Woe!" or "Alas!" Just hugs and kisses and tears of joy that he was home, followed by the excitement of seeing everyone in his father's household rushing to prepare the best party the old house had ever seen.

The old man had been waiting and watching for his son to come to his senses and return home, to be reconciled with him, to take his place in the home where he belonged.

"THIS SON OF YOURS"

A few short hours later, the banquet table was groaning under the weight of bowls and platters overflowing with glorious food, with the perfectly roasted fatted calf in the center of it all. The Prodigal Son had been washed and dressed in soft clothes, and his battered feet bandaged. The village musicians had been called in, the relatives and neighbors were dancing, and the Prodigal Son sat beside his father who would not let go of his boy's hand.

At sundown that day, the first-born son was walking home—alone—after another exhausting day working in the fields. He'd had no help at all from that feckless younger brother who was off somewhere boozing and squandering the family fortune on harlots. As the eldest son reached the crest of a hill, from afar he saw lights blazing in all the windows of his home, and heard the sounds of music and merrymaking. It wasn't a holiday. It wasn't anybody's birthday. What the heck was going on?

When he reached the house, one of the servants enlightened him. "Your brother has come," the servant said, "and your father has killed the fatted calf, because he has received him safe and sound."

That was the last straw. The eldest son raged and bellowed and cursed, swearing that he never wanted to see his rotten kid brother again, and that there was no power on earth that could force him into the house. The servants tried to calm him, all the while pleading that he go in, for his father's sake at least, while another of the servants ran inside to ask for the father's help.

The old man hurried outside, where he discovered that his oldest boy was still in the middle of a major meltdown. He tried to embrace his eldest son, but the boy shook off his father. The old man begged his son to come inside, to welcome his brother home, to join the party, but the first-born was spitting mad. "Lo, these many years I have served you, and I never disobeyed your command; yet you never gave me a kid, that I might make merry with my friends."

Cutting words, but the eldest son wasn't finished. "But when this son of yours came, who has devoured your living with harlots, you killed for him the fatted calf!"

The father bore his eldest son's rebuke as patiently as he had borne his youngest son's selfishness.

"Son," he said, "you are with me always, and all that is mine is yours. It was fitting to make merry and be glad, for this your brother was dead, and is alive; he was lost, and is found."

WHAT THE PRODIGAL SON
can teach us

VIRTUE IS ITS OWN REWARD

The outcome of the Prodigal Son's story fills us with relief, since we know too well how often we have strayed. But there is a part of us that sympathizes strongly with the Prodigal Son's older brother. He had been faithful; he had been good; he had been diligent, hardworking, obedient. He had kept his nose clean. Surely he had delighted his father, so why didn't he ever get a "Thanks for Being a Swell Guy!" party?

"Let us have no self-conceit, no provoking of one another, no envy of one another." (Galatians 5:26)

WE ARE FAMILY

The house could not have been a happy place after the Prodigal Son ran off. His father would have been silent and wretched because his youngest boy had turned his back on him. His older brother would have been angry and resentful not only because of the additional burden the Prodigal's absence placed on him, but also because of the anguish he was causing their father. Over time the older brother's anger and resentment turned into deep bitterness. When the Prodigal repented, apologized, even declared that he didn't deserve to be forgiven, the older brother's heart had grown so cold that he could not rejoice. And by nurturing feelings of hate, he put his own share of the father's estate in jeopardy.

"If one member suffers, all suffer together; if one member is honored, all rejoice together." (1 Corinthians 12:26)

NO HUMAN BEING IS
THE CENTER OF THE UNIVERSE

The Prodigal Son loved being the center of attention, and he thought the only certain way to keep the spotlight on himself was to buy it. He suffered from a warped sense of self and a seriously mistaken notion of what constitutes friendship. The Prodigal Son would pay any price to be the life of the party, and if the people who sponged off him had any feeling for him it was probably envy because he was rich, and perhaps contempt because he was wasting his wealth on people who did not deserve it.

"And you he made alive, when you were dead through the trespasses and sins in which you once walked, following the course of this world, following the prince of the power of the air, the spirit that is now at work in the sons of disobedience. . . . But God, who is rich in mercy, out of the great love with which he loved us, even when we were dead through our trespasses, made us alive together with Christ."
(Ephesians 2:1–2, 4–5)

IT'S NEVER TOO LATE
TO GO HOME TO THE FATHER

The parable of the Prodigal Son teaches a great lesson on God's mercy to sinners, but it is also a lesson in God's generosity to the faithful. Believers who resent it when sinners are forgiven and given a share of the Father's estate put their own inheritance at risk. And in terms of a period of depravity, the Prodigal Son's was short-lived (the fact that the money ran out had a lot to do with that). He turned his life around pretty early on. Compare him to the Good Thief of Luke's gospel who repents as he is dying on the cross. Here he is, after a lifetime of sinful, criminal behavior; when he is minutes away from eternity, he begs for mercy. And he gets it—Christ promises him, "Today you will be with me in paradise."

"And the Lord restored the fortunes of Job . . . and the Lord gave Job twice as much as he had before." (Job 42:10)

THERE ARE LIMITS TO FREEDOM

"It's a free country!"

"It's my choice!"

Invariably, when someone has done or is about to do something that ranges between bad and just plain stupid, they justify their actions with one of these trite expressions. Free will is a gift from God; exercising it is our privilege. Of course, there are plenty of times when we use our free will to make a poor moral choice. The Prodigal Son, puffed up with pride, drunk on his own sense of self-sufficiency, and loaded down with cash, thinks, "Free at last!" and rushes off to mess up his life.

"For freedom Christ has set us free; stand fast therefore, and do not submit again to a yoke of slavery." (Galatians 5:1)

CHAPTER 23

JOHN MARK

SHOULD I STAY OR SHOULD I GO?

Acts 12:12–17
Acts 13:1–13

Mentoring a teenager, even one who is a beloved member of your own family, can be a thankless task. Barnabas discovered just how fickle kids can be when he offered his teenage cousin John Mark the golden opportunity to accompany him and the apostle Paul on a missionary journey. The kid blew it, being too young to appreciate the gift he'd been given. But time passed—and the experience of his youth had a remarkable impact on John Mark's adulthood.

Offering a teenager a career-building opportunity is not likely to bring an adult instant gratification. A teen's attention span is short. The number of competing distractions is legion. Kids are full of overconfidence one day, and plunged into the depths of self-doubt the next. And let's not even get into the subject of oversleeping. So when kind-hearted Barnabas invited his young cousin John Mark along on a missionary journey with Paul, the apostle was willing to give the boy a chance and agreed that he could accompany them. But John Mark blew it, irritating Paul, and ultimately breaking up Paul's and Barnabas' friendship.

John Mark came from a distinguished Christian family, one of the first to accept the gospel in Jerusalem. His mother, Mary, had a fine house in the city, large enough to serve as a meeting place for Christians. When Herod had Peter arrested, the leading Christians of Jerusalem gathered at Mary's house to pray for the apostle, and discuss what they ought to do—Herod had already executed James; Peter was likely to meet the same end. Should they flee persecution, or remain in Jerusalem and bear witness to the gospel by their martyrdom?

As the discussion dragged on into the night, there came a soft knock at the gate. Rhoda, the house's doorkeeper, called through the bolted gate, "Who is it?" A man replied, "Rhoda, it is Peter."

In her excitement, Rhoda left Peter outside while she rushed into the house to declare that Peter was at the gate. The assembly would not believe her. "You are mad!" some of them exclaimed. But Rhoda insisted, and so they followed her out, across the courtyard toward the entrance. They could hear someone knocking. This time Rhoda turned the key and threw open the door. There, in the shadows of the porch, wrapped in his mantle, stood Peter. Everyone cried out in joy at the sight of him, but with a gesture of his hand Peter silenced them—it would do no good to draw attention to the house, or to the fact that Herod's prize prisoner had escaped. Speaking quickly, Peter described how an angel of the Lord had rescued him. Then, unwilling to put Mary and John Mark in danger, he went off into the night to hide in the home of a less prominent Christian family.

A SON OF THE DEVIL

After the excitement of Peter's miraculous deliverance from Herod's prison (followed by Herod's predictable execution of the unhappy prison guards), Paul and Barnabas planned a missionary journey—Paul's first—to Antioch, the island of Cyprus, and to the city of Perga in Pamphylia (in what is now Turkey). Barnabas lobbied hard to take along his teenage cousin, John Mark. The boy would be a useful general assistant, Barnabas argued, and given his family's standing in the Christian community of Jerusalem, it was only a matter of time before John Mark would begin preaching the gospel, too. Eventually, he would probably hold a leadership position among the Christians.

Given all these considerations, bringing John Mark along would be excellent training for such a promising young man.

Paul agreed to give John Mark a chance, and the three set out for Antioch. From Antioch they caught a ship to Cyprus, and there John Mark saw firsthand what was involved in building up the church. They traveled over the entire island, an area of over 3,500 square miles, preaching primarily in the synagogues—experience at home had taught Paul and Barnabas that their fellow Jews were most open to the message that Jesus was the fulfillment of the words of the prophets. But news of the strangers and their teachings spread among the Gentiles of Cyprus, too.

At Paphos, one of the main cities of Cyprus, the Roman proconsul, Segius Paulus, summoned the missionaries to tell him about Jesus. This was a golden opportunity to convert the most important man on Cyprus, and Paul was hoping for the best. Accompanied by Barnabas and John Mark, the apostle presented himself at Sergius Paulus' villa. The trio had tidied themselves up for the occasion, washing themselves and putting on clean clothes, but Paul, Barnabas, and John Mark could not hide what they were—two relatively poor men and a teenage boy from an unsophisticated backwater of the Roman Empire. Fortunately, their humble appearance was not a liability: Romans and Greeks expected philosophers to be dressed simply.

The steward of the villa escorted Paul, Barnabas, and John Mark into the proconsul's audience hall. There, they found Sergius Paulus dressed in a dazzling white woolen toga and seated upon a white marble chair that looked very much like a throne. The proconsul was not alone; standing beside his chair was a sorcerer and false prophet who called himself Bar-Jesus. As Paul began to explain the gospel message, Bar-Jesus kept interrupting, contradicting everything the apostle said, and doing his utmost to persuade Sergius Paulus to reject Christianity and get rid of the missionaries.

And now things got exciting. Paul turned on Bar-Jesus, staring him down, then said, "You son of the devil, you enemy of all righteousness, full of all deceit and villainy, will you not stop making crooked the straight paths of the Lord?" John Mark had never seen Paul filled with righteous anger. Neither had Bar-Jesus, of course, and as the sorcerer stood there, a smug expression on his face, Paul raised his hands and declared, "And now, behold, the hand of the Lord is upon you, and you shall be blind and unable to see the sun for a time." Immediately, Bar-Jesus was struck blind. Crying in dismay, he staggered about the hall, calling on Sergius Paulus' attendants to help him. As for the proconsul, he was astonished by what he had just witnessed. The miracle, combined with the message of the gospel, convinced him to convert to Christianity.

MR. UNRELIABLE

Perga in the first century A.D. was a magnificent city, unlike anything John Mark ever would have known. Compared to this Greco-Roman metropolis, Jerusalem was a dusty village in the Judean boondocks. Founded by the Greeks and expanded and improved upon by the Romans, Perga had a magnificent outdoor theater that could accommodate 14,000 spectators. There was also a stadium, where enormous crowds cheered for their favorite charioteer at the races and their favorite gladiator as he battled men or wild beasts. As for the religious center of Perga, it was the magnificent Temple of Artemis, dedicated to Apollo's twin sister, the goddess of the moon and of the hunt. Christianity had not made a dent in Perga, but Paul and Barnabas were eager to change that.

The missionaries had barely begun their work evangelizing the people of Perga when John Mark announced he was going home. Barnabas was speechless. Paul was livid. As a favor to Barnabas he had agreed that the boy could travel with them. He had included him in every aspect of their mission, even taking him along to Sergius Paulus' villa where the boy had witnessed the miracle that blinded

Bar-Jesus and brought about the conversion of the Roman proconsul. World travel. Witnessing miracles. Rubbing elbows with high Roman officials. What teenage boy back in Jerusalem had such opportunities? None, of course, but this ungrateful, inconstant little puppy found the work too hard, or the food too strange, or the weather too hot, or the unpredictability of missionary work too unsettling or too boring. And so he quit.

Barnabas tried to talk John Mark out of leaving—after all, his own reputation with Paul was on the line. Barnabas was the one who had persuaded Paul to take the boy along. But John Mark, sullen and feeling a touch guilty, wouldn't listen to his cousin's appeals. Paul's admonition, "Go! And good riddance!" at least let John Mark off the hook.

By scurrying home to Mommy, John Mark missed the great conversion of the Gentiles in Antioch, the healing of the man who had been crippled since birth, and Paul's and Barnabas' dramatic if disconcerting experience in Lystra where the pagans of the city assumed Barnabas was Zeus, king of the gods, and Paul was Hermes, messenger of the gods, and prepared to sacrifice oxen to the them. All in all, for a first missionary journey, it was an encouraging beginning—no thanks to that unreliable kid, John Mark.

A BROKEN FRIENDSHIP

When Paul and Barnabas returned to Jerusalem, John Mark stayed out of sight. Why embarrass his cousin further, or expose himself to another tongue lashing from Paul? But the rest of the church in Jerusalem was eager to hear the news of the founding of communities of Christians in Cyprus and Pamphylia.

As it happened, Paul and Barnabas arrived just in time to participate in a major discussion among the church leadership about whether Gentile converts should be circumcised. Paul and Barnabas assured the congregation that the gospel was well received among the Gentiles, but they warned that insisting that all men and boys who wanted to be baptized must also be circumcised was likely to depress the conversion rate significantly. Peter agreed, and so did James.

Having settled the question regarding Gentile converts, Paul was eager to begin a second missionary journey. "Come," he said to Barnabas, "let us return and visit the brethren in every city where we proclaimed the word of the Lord, and see how they are." Barnabas agreed that this was a fine idea, and suggested they should take John Mark along with them again.

That was too much for Paul. Hadn't Barnabas been paying attention when John Mark, finding missionary work too tedious, had abandoned them and scampered home? Paul flat-out refused to permit John Mark to join them again. Barnabas got defensive; Paul became angrier. The climax came when Barnabas threw down a "Preach with me, preach with my cousin" challenge. Paul replied that he would not travel so far as across the street with that feckless, ungrateful, undependable, snot-nosed kid.

At that, Paul and Barnabas split up, and never worked together again. Barnabas, with John Mark in tow, sailed to Cyprus. Paul recruited another disciple, Silas, to join him on a journey to Syria and Cilicia, a beautiful region along the Aegean Sea in what is now southern Turkey.

A SECOND CHANCE

But it didn't end there. About a decade later (c. 60 A.D.), when Paul was imprisoned in Rome, he wrote to the Christians of Colossae, "Aristarchus my fellow prisoner greets you, and Mark the cousin of Barnabas (concerning whom you have received instructions—if he comes to you, receive him)." (Colossians 4:10)

What could be plainer? John Mark had grown up and even had been able to redeem himself in Paul's eyes, becoming one of the apostle's closest disciples. The unpleasantness in Pamphylia was forgotten because John Mark had matured—so much so that he had followed Paul to Rome to serve him while he was in prison. About the same time, in his letter to Philemon, Paul passed along Mark's greetings to one of the foremost of the Colossian converts. Finally, shortly before his martyrdom, Paul wrote to Timothy, urging him to "Get Mark and bring him with you; for he is very useful in serving me." (2 Timothy 4:11)

What a change! The petulant, unreliable teenager Paul couldn't stand to have near him had grown up to be one of Paul's most dependable disciples. Assuming that Timothy did bring Mark to Rome with him, they probably both witnessed Paul's execution, and almost certainly took part in burying him on the Via Ostia outside the walls of Rome.

There was another apostle in Rome at this time—Peter. Writing to the Christians in Asia Minor, Peter refers to himself being in "Babylon," his metaphor for Nero's Rome. In his letter he said that all the Christians of Rome sent their fellow Christians greetings, "and so does my son Mark." Astonishing. John Mark had won the admiration, trust, and affection of the two greatest apostles. But he went on to become famous in his own right, as the author of the Gospel of Mark.

It just goes to show you—even the most irresponsible teenager can turn out well.

WHAT JOHN MARK
can teach us

SPIRITUAL GROWTH TAKES TIME—
AND EFFORT

When John Mark was an adolescent boy, his character, not to mention his attention span, had some growing to do. That's not uncommon among teenagers. But in time, he did grow to be a responsible young man, even winning over Paul and becoming indispensable to the great apostle. In addition to a more mature character, John Mark also experienced spiritual growth; he matured as a man and as a Christian.

The way to jump-start our own spiritual growth is to set time aside for prayer, for reflecting on the Bible, and for serving our neighbors and our church. It's demanding, and it requires discipline, but in the end such a commitment leads to a closer relationship with the Lord.

"And we desire each of you to show the same earnestness in realizing the full assurance of hope until the end, so that you may not be sluggish, but imitators of those who through faith and patience inherit the promises." (Hebrews 6:11–12)

NOBODY LIKES A COMMITMENT-PHOBE

We've all met irritating individuals who chatter on interminably about their quest for the perfect spouse, the perfect job, the perfect church community. Yet nothing and no one ever seems to be good enough for them; there's always some issue that prevents them from making a commitment. Such behavior is not an example of someone with very high standards; it is a defense against committing to a person and beginning a life-long romance, or taking a job that could lead to a rewarding career, or joining a church that will feed the soul.

In any situation there will be disappointments and even failures, but these are just speed bumps on the journey. Use your best judgment before you make a serious commitment, and once you have, turn to the Lord to help you remain faithful.

"But I will not remove from him my steadfast love, or be false to my faithfulness. I will not violate my covenant, or alter the word that went forth from my lips." (Psalm 89:33–34)

THERE'S A DIFFERENCE BETWEEN BEING CHILDLIKE AND CHILDISH

A person who is childlike is innocent, trusting, honest, and open to meeting new people, learning new things, and taking on new challenges and experiences. Someone who is childish is selfish, impulsive, fickle, and undependable. As a teenager John Mark was still in the childish stage, but he outgrew it and gave up all the unattractive qualities associated with childishness. Paul welcomed the mature John Mark into his inner circle of friends and disciples because he understood what it takes to make the transition from child to adult.

"When I was a child, I spoke like a child, I thought like a child, I reasoned like a child; when I became a man, I gave up childish ways." (1 Corinthians 11)

NOTHING'S IMPOSSIBLE—
ANYBODY CAN CHANGE

Slamming on the brakes and altering the direction of your life is
never easy, but it can be done. And if and when you decide to make a
change for the better, the Lord will be your most constant supporter.
But the change has to be genuine. Lip service to change won't do.
If you find that you've settled into certain patterns of behavior with
your family, your coworkers, or your fellow Christians that are lifeless,
unloving, perhaps even flat-out bad, then it is time for renewal.

*"Therefore, if anyone is in Christ, he is a new creation; the old has
passed away, behold, the new has come." (2 Corinthians 5:17)*

CHAPTER 24

BERNICE

QUEEN OF DENIAL

Acts 25

If, as they say, the apple doesn't fall far from the tree, it's not surprising that Bernice, a descendant of the notorious King Herod, should have had an unsavory reputation. Bad luck to be widowed twice as a young woman; bad judgment to take up with her brother. Lacking respect for the laws of man and God, could Bernice have been surprised that she was not a beloved monarch?

J acob's sons were a headache. David's elder sons couldn't be trusted. Ahab's and Jezebel's children were nightmares. But for consistent depravity, you can't beat the Herodian dynasty that we encounter in the New Testament. From generation to generation, the Herodian children followed in the family tradition of cruelty and depravity, and one of the Depravity All-Stars was Bernice.

Let's go back to the founder of the line, Herod, known as "the Great": he was the king who massacred the baby boys of Bethlehem in an attempt to kill to the Christ Child. This Herod also murdered his wife, his brother-in-law, and four of his sons.

Herod the Great's granddaughter, Herodias, married one of her uncles, divorced him, then married another uncle. As a reward for a particularly captivating dance, Herodias' daughter, Salome, requested—and received—the head of John the Baptist on a platter.

Herodias' brother, Herod Agrippa I, executed the apostle James, and imprisoned Peter. When he began to pretend that he was a living god, an angel of the Lord struck him down. (Acts 12:19–23)

*If her Daddy thought he was a god, you can imagine
what Bernice must have been like as a little girl: a high-
maintenance child, willful, fickle, refusing to do anything which she found difficult or unpleasant, defying
the nurses who were assigned to bring her up, and pitching tantrums at a decibel level that could crack marble.*

Bernice (sometimes spelled Berenice) was the daughter of Herod
Agrippa I, and very much in the mold of her notorious family. If her
Daddy thought he was a god, you can imagine what Bernice must
have been like as a little girl: a high-maintenance child, willful, fickle,
refusing to do anything that she found difficult or unpleasant, defying the nurses who were assigned to bring her up, and pitching tantrums at a decibel level that could crack marble. It makes you pity
the unfortunate country that got Bernice as their queen.

THE BLACK WIDOW

Bernice was about 22 when her family married her off to a man
named Marcus Julius Alexander. In spite of his name, Marcus and his
family were not Romans, but Jewish. But ambition meant more to
Marcus's family than religion, and by the time Marcus married Bernice, he and the rest of his family had either abandoned the practice
of their ancestral faith completely, or completely neglected it.

Finding Bernice a Jewish husband was not important in her family either. Marcus' primary appeal was his family's ties to the emperor
in Rome. The Emperor Claudius (of *I, Claudius* fame) favored this
clan. They already held important government posts in Alexandria,
and Marcus or his brother stood poised someday to become the

Roman governor of Egypt. Alas, the marriage of Marcus and Bernice didn't last long; after three years, Marcus died.

By Bernice's day it had become a tradition among the Herodian ladies that when they went husband-shopping, they looked first at their uncles. And Bernice was no different. Her husband Marcus' funeral pyre was still smoldering when she married her uncle Herod of Chalcis.

With Herod of Chalcis, Bernice had two sons. The boys were still infants when their father died; Bernice was beginning to get a reputation as the Black Widow of Judea. She hadn't killed off her husbands, but she did seem to bring them the worst kind of luck.

BROTHERLY LOVE

This time Bernice did not rush into marriage. And instead of looking for company among her uncles, she turned to her brother, Herod Agrippa II. Brother and sister lived together as husband and wife in their palace in Caesarea, a town Herod the Great had built on the shores of the Mediterranean Sea. Jerusalem, the real capital of Judea, was hot, choked with dust, filled with religious and political zealots. Caesarea was cooled by breezes from the sea, and unlike Jerusalem, it was a city in the Roman style. An aqueduct brought fresh water to Caesarea from Mount Carmel. There were luxurious public baths, and a grand forum. For entertainment, Bernice and Agrippa could watch Greek tragedies or lewd Roman farces at the Theater, cheer for their favorite team at the chariot races in the Hippodrome, or watch gladiators battle wild beasts—or each other—in the Amphitheater. Of course, these were all pagan amusements, unsuitable for devout Jews, but the Herodians had always been only barely Jewish, never devout.

The scandal of Bernice's and Agrippa's love affair would have set off bloody riots in the streets had they lived in Jerusalem. In Caesarea, however, the residents were more tolerant. Nonetheless, as time went on, there was subtle pressure on the royal couple to give up their incestuous relationship, which made them if not a scandal, an object of dirty jokes in the other royal courts around the Mediterranean. The obvious solution was a new marriage for Bernice—her third.

Her new husband was Polemon II, king of Cilicia. Bernice liked waterfront real estate, and Cilicia occupied a lovely stretch of the southern coast of Turkey, overlooking the turquoise waters of the Aegean Sea. The climate was mild, the land was fertile, the kingdom was rich. And in addition to being king, Polemon was descended from Mark Antony—Bernice was marrying into one of the most distinguished families in the Roman Empire.

All these advantages did not matter, however; the couple could not get along. After two or three years together, Bernice had the marriage dissolved and moved back to Caesarea where her brother Agrippa was waiting.

RELATIVELY PEACEFUL

Bernice had not been back in Caesarea long when trouble—BIG trouble—erupted in Jerusalem. In 64 A.D., Nero appointed a man named Gessius Florus to govern Judea. Florus's primary qualification for the job was that he was an intimate friend of Nero's wife, Poppaea, a woman who knew more about intrigue and ruthlessness than Bernice ever would.

Judea was a touchy province to govern, as Pontius Pilate learned. The Jews would not permit any statue or carving of any kind in Jerusalem, not even a sculpture of the emperor. The Temple was sacrosanct, and even the Roman governor could not enter it. And anything belonging to the Temple was also holy, since the Jews regarded it as the property of God. As long as these prohibitions were respected, Judea would remain peaceful. Relatively speaking. But if a Roman governor tried to throw his weight around, the Jews were ready to defend their faith with their lives.

Florus was an arrogant little stinker who, as he saw it, was not about to let the Jews push him around. In Caesarea he gave preferential treatment to the pagan Greeks of the city at the expense of Caesarea's Jewish community. The Greeks noticed that they were high in Florus's favor, so one Saturday morning, as the Jews of the town were worshipping in their synagogue, a Greek troublemaker sacrificed several birds to the gods at the entrance to the Jewish holy place. The Jews were outraged at this provocation, not least because it rendered their synagogue ritually unclean.

A delegation of distinguished Jewish men of Caesarea appealed to Florus for justice. As the man had a reputation for looking most favorably on petitioners who gave him a gift, the Jews of Caesarea presented Florus with eight talents of gold (as bribes go, this was a small fortune—one talent weighed about 75 pounds). Florus heard the Jews' petition, accepted their "gift," then ordered his guards to lock up the entire delegation. The Jews of Caesarea seethed with anger and resentment, but as a minority community in a great Roman metropolis there was nothing to do, other than to swallow their pride along with their indignation and submit.

Having stirred up division in Caesarea, Florus traveled south to Jerusalem to see what trouble he could make there. In the holy city, he forced his way into the Temple treasury, where he removed seventeen talents of gold. The talents, he claimed, were for back taxes owed to the emperor.

Outraged, the Jews of Jerusalem took to the streets to protest this sacrilegious theft. Florus responded by arresting the leading men of the city; he had them whipped, then crucified.

With the entire province on the brink of rebellion, Bernice hurried down to Jerusalem to talk sense to Florus. Heaven knows she was not religious, but Judea was her province, and if the Romans marched in to crush a Jewish uprising, her income, her privileges, her authority

BAD KIDS OF THE BIBLE

would be crushed with it. But Florus would not listen to Bernice. From his perspective, the Jews demanded too much from Rome and gave back too little. They must be brought to heel like every other conquered province under Roman rule.

THE INVASION

Having gotten nowhere with the Roman, Bernice urged her brother Agrippa to appeal to the Jewish people. Weeping to show his earnestness, Agrippa begged his people to keep the peace. But the people of Judea had nothing but hatred and contempt for Agrippa and Bernice, whom they regarded as a pair of incestuous pagans. The crowd's response to Agrippa's appeal was memorable: They rioted, and burned down Agrippa's and Bernice's palace.

Brother and sister were hopelessly corrupt, but they weren't stupid. They fled north to the safety of Galilee and waited for the inevitable—a Roman invasion.

The Romans invaded Judea in 66, led by Vespasian, a successful general whose conquests in Britain had made him a legend in Rome. With 60,000 veteran Roman legionnaires, and assisted by his eldest son, 27-year-old Titus, Vespasian conquered Galilee, then turned toward Jerusalem. But while the legionnaires were subduing Galilee, Titus and Bernice had become lovers.

Titus was ten years younger than Bernice. He was on the short side, but handsome and physically powerful. Surprisingly for a soldier, he played the harp and sang well; he also wrote poetry. On the battlefield, he was an expert horseman, and skilled with the Roman short sword and with the bow. Bernice was smitten with him. As for Titus, he was intoxicated by this exotic, notorious queen who had run through three husbands and conducted a long-running affair with her own brother. There is a story that while the Romans were still busy subduing the Jewish rebels in Galilee, Bernice traveled to Jerusalem with Titus to give him a tour. There, holding his hand, she walked him through the precincts of the Temple, and even into the sanctuary itself. It may or may not be true, but it does sound like the type of thoughtless thing Bernice would do.

BACKING THE RIGHT HORSE

As the love affair between Bernice and Titus heated up, so did the war in Judea. And making things more complicated but also more interesting was a volatile political situation in Rome. In 68, the enemies of Emperor Nero joined forces to destroy him. Uprisings broke out in Gaul; the Roman Senate voted to name Galba, governor of Spain, emperor; and the Praetorians, the emperor's personal bodyguards, were bribed to kill him. Nero ran for his life, but not fast enough. The Praetorians were about to overtake him when, with the help of his secretary, the fugitive emperor stabbed himself to death.

With Nero dead, the empire turned chaotic. The Senate may have wanted Galba as emperor, but there were three other contenders, each of whom felt he was better qualified to rule the world. One of these candidates was Vespasian. The idea of her future father-in-law being emperor of Rome appealed to Bernice; she gave Vespasian an enormous amount of gold to help him raise an army large enough to defeat his rivals and seize Rome.

While Vespasian pursued a crown in Italy, Titus took over the siege of Jerusalem. It was a bitter fight, and the Jewish defenders put up a heroic resistance. At one point a skirmishing party from the city almost succeeded in capturing Titus. In the end, famine undermined the defenses of Jerusalem. The Romans broke through the city walls, and every street and alley in the city became a battlefield. The survivors barricaded themselves inside the Temple, but the Romans battered down the massive gates, massacred the defenders, looted the sanctuary of all its sacred vessels, and set fire to the Temple. The

Jewish historian Josephus, who was an eyewitness to the Roman destruction of Judea, estimated that the Romans killed one million people in and around Jerusalem, and carried off 97,000 as slaves.

None of this troubled Bernice. She was in the fleet of ships that carried the loot of the Temple and thousands of weeping captives to Rome. Her countrymen were heading to the slave markets; Bernice was heading to Titus's palace where, any day now, she expected to become his wife. And since Vespasian had succeeded in his bid to become emperor, Bernice was in line to become Rome's next empress.

Bernice lived happily in Titus's palace in Rome. She acted his wife; he treated her as if she were his wife; people who wanted favors from Titus appealed to Bernice for help just as they would appeal to the wife of any man of wealth and influence. But Titus still hadn't proposed marriage.

That was puzzling to Bernice, but not to Titus. Romans did not like the idea of a foreign woman becoming empress. To keep the love of the Roman people, Julius Caesar had tried to hush up his love affair with Cleopatra. And he was wise to do so, because a few years later, when Mark Antony took up with Cleopatra and made no effort at all to hide the affair, the people of Rome turned against him. There were parallels between Cleopatra and Bernice: Both were queens from the East; both were notorious for their sexual exploits; and both were older than their Roman lovers.

The end of the affair came in an unexpected way: Actors in the theaters of Rome began making jokes about Titus and Bernice. A future emperor could not afford to be an object of mockery, and Titus sent Bernice back to Caesarea.

We don't know what happened to Bernice after she and Titus split up. We know that her brother/boyfriend Agrippa II lived until 92, but all trace of Bernice has vanished from the historical record. Perhaps she lived long enough to see Titus become emperor, and then die after barely two years on the throne. Bernice would have liked that.

WHAT BERNICE
can teach us

RESPECT THE SANCTITY OF THE FAMILY

Yes, we are stating the obvious here, but it's worth repeating: incest undermines the sanctity of marriage, the family structure, and the stability of society. The fact that it can produce physical, emotional, and mental disabilities in the children of incestuous relationships underscores the idea that nature herself is against it. A glance through Leviticus and Deuteronomy reveals that God hates incest.

"Let marriage be held in honor among all, and let the marriage bed
be undefiled; for God will judge the immoral and the adulterous."
(Hebrews 13:4)

DO NOT SIDE WITH THE WICKED
AGAINST THE INNOCENT

Time and again we see how the worst people gain the upper hand and the good suffer. There are even circumstances when standing up for what is right, when defending those who are innocent against those who abuse them can make you a target. Nonetheless, the law of God is clear: It is wrong to follow the example of Bernice and side with the unjust against the just.

"It is not good to be partial to a wicked man, or to deprive a righteous
man of justice." (Proverbs 18:5)

RESPECT WHAT OTHER PEOPLE CONSIDER HOLY

There is a book, *How to Be a Perfect Guest*, which explains how to conduct yourself when in a house of worship that is not your own. Bernice's and Titus's stroll through the Temple was an act of gross insensitivity. Worse, it was a flagrant sign of contempt for the religious sensibilities of the Jews—particularly on the part of Bernice, who as a woman who was nominally Jewish knew how deeply this would offend her people. Who among us would commit acts of sacrilege or vandalism against a holy place? But some would allow gross rudeness more leeway. You don't have to agree with how your neighbors pray, but if you have been invited to a service in their house of worship, act respectfully. If that is beyond you, then stay away and join the party later.

> *"I dwell in the high and holy place, and also with him who is of a contrite and humble spirit." (Isaiah 57:15)*

ACKNOWLEDGMENTS

My sincerest thanks to my friends at Fair Winds Press—Will Kiester, John Gettings, Cara Connors, and Tiffany Hill. And my special thanks to Bernadette Baczynski, a perceptive editor and a fine writer who made countless improvements to this book. Will, John, Cara, Tiffany, Bernadette—I am in your debt.

ABOUT THE AUTHOR

Thomas J. Craughwell is the author of more than a dozen books, most recently *Stealing Lincoln's Body* and *Saints Behaving Badly*. He has written articles on history, religion, politics, and popular culture for the *Wall Street Journal*, the *American Spectator*, and *U.S. News & World Report*. He lives in Bethel, Connecticut.

A

295

BAD KIDS OF THE BIBLE